plays
to
remember

LITERATURE TO ENJOY
STORIES TO ENJOY
POEMS TO ENJOY
PLAYS TO ENJOY
READINGS TO ENJOY

LITERATURE TO REMEMBER
STORIES TO REMEMBER
POEMS TO REMEMBER
PLAYS TO REMEMBER
READINGS TO REMEMBER

plays to remember

HENRY B. MALONEY
University of Detroit

MACMILLAN PUBLISHING COMPANY
NEW YORK

COLLIER MACMILLAN PUBLISHERS
LONDON

ACKNOWLEDGMENTS

For permission to reprint copyright material in this volume, grateful acknowledgment is made to the following:

University of London Press, Ltd.: For *The Jewels of the Shrine* by James Ene Henshaw. From *Plays of Black Africa*, edited by Frederic M. Litto. Reprinted by permission of University of London Press, Ltd.

Dramatists Play Service, Inc.: For *Sorry, Wrong Number* by Lucille Fletcher. Copyright 1952, 1948 by Lucille Fletcher. All rights reserved under the International and Pan American Conventions. Reprinted by permission of Margaret Sherman, Dramatists Play Service, Inc.
This play is to be used only for study. Written permission for any kind of public performance must be obtained from Dramatists Play Service, Inc., 440 Park Avenue, South, New York, N.Y. 10016.

Grove Press, Inc., and Calder and Boyars Ltd.: For *The Leader*, by Eugene Ionesco, translated by Derek Prouse. Copyright © 1960 by John Calder Ltd. Reprinted by permission of Judith Schmidt, Grove Press, Inc., and Marion Boyars, Calder and Boyars Ltd. Published in France by Editions Gallimard, 1958.

The Harold Matson Company, Inc.: For *The Meadow* by Ray Bradbury. Copyright © 1966 by Ray Bradbury. Reprinted by permission of Edna M. Pearce, The Harold Matson Company, Inc.

McIntosh and Otis, Inc.: For *The Leader of the People* by John Steinbeck. Copyright 1938 from the book *The Red Pony*, copyright © 1952 by John Steinbeck. Based upon the story "The Leader of the People," dramatized by Luella E. McMahon. Reprinted by permission of Elizabeth R. Otis, McIntosh and Otis, Inc.

(acknowledgments continued on page 210)

NOTE: Amateurs and professionals are warned that *none* of the plays reprinted in this book may be acted, read in public, or presented as a radio or television broadcast without special permission of the author or his agent.

Illustrated by Shannon Stirnweis and Douglas Jamieson

Macmillan Publishing Company
866 Third Avenue, New York, New York 10022
Collier Macmillan Canada, Inc.
Printed in the United States of America

CONTENTS

Everybody Wants to Get into the Act

Many years ago a popular comedian performed a routine that audiences loved. He would sit at a piano and begin to play. Soon a woman would walk on stage and interrupt him. The comedian would begin to play again until being interrupted by a second woman. He would start to play a third time. Finally a man would come on stage and interrupt the comedian, who would then turn to the audience in frustration and cry, "Everybody wants to get into the act!"

This routine was so popular with audiences because they recognized a truth in it. They knew that, indeed, many people do like to get into the act. Perhaps the comedian's routine reminded them of a time when they themselves were interrupted by others. You may also recall a situation when other people bothered you when you wished to be left alone.

Although people like to "get into the act," not everyone does it in the same way. Only a few individuals actually possess the talent or desire to be a performer on stage. The rest of us are satisfied by watching them perform. We watch plays in the theater and on television. Or we can "get into the act" by reading plays in a book.

This book is a collection of plays for your reading pleasure. Most of the selections are one-act plays. Because they are short, the playwright must get the action of the play started immediately. Your job is to read carefully in order not to miss any important details that will help you understand and appreciate the play. Those details begin with the very first pages of the play. Start by reading the list of characters in the story. After each name there may be an indication of each individual's occupation or relationship to another character. Next study the details of time and place. Note exactly when and where the action takes place. Try to picture in your mind the setting as the playwright has imagined it.

Also be sure to pay attention to all descriptions of characters. Picture their faces, their ages, their clothing. As each character speaks, think about the kind of individual that speaker seems to be. Look for stage directions that indicate the emotions with which characters talk. In addition, pay attention to comments that other characters make about an individual. Their remarks can help you understand a particular personality. After you become familiar with each person in the play, you will be prepared to get involved with their problems.

As you read further into a play, try to visualize all the action as it might occur on stage. Even if the play you read is a radio play, picture how the characters would move if the story occurred on a stage. Think of yourself as a quiet bystander standing near the actors.

Above all, give the play your full concentration. If you are reading a mystery story, you will feel the chills and suspense as the action unfolds. If the play is a comedy, you will appreciate the humor and unexpected turns in the plot. Whatever the type of play, you can get the most out of your reading by giving your undivided attention.

At the end of each play, you will find discussion questions and suggested topics for composition. Think about the total effect the play has had on you before you complete these activities. Consider the development of the action and how the characters behaved. Think about which characters changed the most by the end of the play. Ask yourself which characters you admired most and least in the story, and try to find reasons for your opinions. Finally, think about the things that made the play end as it did. Pinpoint the most important events in the story. By doing all this, you will have taken advantage of the richness that reading plays has to offer.

SORRY, WRONG NUMBER

LUCILLE FLETCHER

SORRY, WRONG NUMBER

Have you ever accidentally overheard a conversation that was not meant for your ears? Suppose you overhear two people discussing a crime that is about to be committed. What should you do?

In *Sorry, Wrong Number* you will discover what Mrs. Elbert Stevenson does when she happens to hear such a conversation. Since Mrs. Stevenson is an invalid, she cannot run out to the nearest police station. She must depend on her telephone.

Although *Sorry, Wrong Number* was made into a movie and has been performed on the stage, it was originally a radio play. Consequently, it relies heavily on sounds to get across its dramatic punch. As you read, imagine the ringing, buzzing, clicking, and dialing of Mrs. Stevenson's telephone. Imagine, too, what kind of mood she is in when she slams down the receiver.

Listen. Mrs. Stevenson is just beginning to dial.

CHARACTERS

MRS. STEVENSON

OPERATOR

FIRST MAN

SECOND MAN (GEORGE)

CHIEF OPERATOR

SECOND OPERATOR

SERGEANT DUFFY

THIRD OPERATOR

WESTERN UNION MAN

INFORMATION OPERATOR

WOMAN, on staff of Henchley Hospital

(Sound: Number being dialed on phone; busy signal.)

MRS. STEVENSON *(a querulous, self-centered neurotic).* Oh—
dear! *(Slams down receiver. Dials* OPERATOR.*)*

OPERATOR. Your call, please?

MRS. STEVENSON. Operator? I've been dialing Murray Hill
4-0098 now for the last three-quarters of an hour, and the
line is always busy. But I don't see how it *could* be busy
that long. Will you try it for me, please?

OPERATOR. Murray Hill 4-0098? One moment, please.

MRS. STEVENSON. I don't see how it could be busy all this time.
It's my husband's office. He's working late tonight, and I'm
all alone here in the house. My health is very poor—and
I've been feeling so nervous all day—

OPERATOR. Ringing Murray Hill 4-0098.

*(Sound: Phone buzz. It rings three times. Receiver is picked
up at other end.)*

FIRST MAN. Hello.

MRS. STEVENSON. Hello? *(A little puzzled.)* Hello. Is Mr.
Stevenson there?

FIRST MAN (*into phone, as though he had not heard*). Hello. (*Louder.*) Hello.

SECOND MAN (*slow, heavy quality, faintly foreign accent*). Hello.

FIRST MAN. Hello. George?

GEORGE. Yes, sir.

MRS. STEVENSON (*louder and more imperious, to phone*). Hello. Who's this? What number am I calling, please?

FIRST MAN. We have heard from our client. He says the coast is clear for tonight.

GEORGE. Yes, sir.

FIRST MAN. Where are you now?

GEORGE. In a phone booth.

FIRST MAN. Okay. You know the address. At eleven o'clock the private patrolman goes around to the bar on Second Avenue for a beer. Be sure that all the lights downstairs are out. There should be only one light visible from the street. At eleven fifteen a subway train crosses the bridge. It makes a noise in case her window is open and she should scream.

MRS. STEVENSON (*shocked*). Oh—*hello!* What number is this, please?

GEORGE. Okay. I understand.

FIRST MAN. Make it quick. As little blood as possible. Our client does not wish to make her suffer long.

GEORGE. A knife okay, sir?

FIRST MAN. Yes. A knife will be okay. And remember—remove the rings and bracelets, and the jewelry in the bureau drawer. Our client wishes it to look like simple robbery.

GEORGE. Okay, I get—
(*Sound: A bland buzzing signal.*)

MRS. STEVENSON (*clicking phone*). Oh! (*Bland buzzing signal continues. She hangs up.*) How awful! How unspeakably—
(*Sound: Dialing. Phone buzz.*)

OPERATOR. Your call, please?

MRS. STEVENSON (*unnerved and breathless, into phone*). Operator, I—I've just been cut off.

OPERATOR. I'm sorry, madam. What number were you calling?

MRS. STEVENSON. Why—it was supposed to be Murray Hill 4-0098, but it wasn't. Some wires must have crossed—I was cut into a wrong number—and—I've just heard the most dreadful thing—a—a murder—and—(*Imperiously.*) Operator, you'll simply have to retrace that call at once.

OPERATOR. I beg your pardon, madam—I don't quite—

MRS. STEVENSON. Oh—I know it was a wrong number, and I had no business listening—but these two men—they were cold-blooded fiends—and they were going to murder somebody—some poor innocent woman—who was all alone—in a house near a bridge. And we've got to stop them—we've got to—

OPERATOR (*patiently*). What number were you calling, madam?

MRS. STEVENSON. That doesn't matter. This was a wrong number. And *you* dialed it. And we've got to find out what it was—immediately!

OPERATOR. But—madam—

MRS. STEVENSON. Oh, why are you so stupid? Look, it was obviously a case of some little slip of the finger. I told you to try Murray Hill 4-0098 for me—you dialed it—but your finger must have slipped—and I was connected with some other number—and I could hear them, but they couldn't hear me. Now I simply fail to see why you couldn't make that same mistake again—on purpose—why you couldn't *try* to dial Murray Hill 4-0098 in the same careless sort of way.

OPERATOR (*quickly*). Murray Hill 4-0098? I will try to get it for you, madam.

MRS. STEVENSON (*sarcastically*). Thank you.

(*Sound of dialing; busy signal.*)

OPERATOR. I am sorry. Murray Hill 4-0098 is busy.

MRS. STEVENSON (*frantically clicking receiver*). Operator. Operator.

OPERATOR. Yes, madam.

MRS. STEVENSON (*angrily*). You *didn't* try to get that wrong number at all. I asked explicitly. And all you did was dial correctly.

OPERATOR. I am sorry. What number were you calling?

MRS. STEVENSON. Can't you, for once, forget what number I was calling, and do something specific? Now I want to trace that call. It's my civic duty—it's *your* civic duty—to trace that call—and to apprehend those dangerous killers—and if *you* won't—

OPERATOR. I will connect you with the Chief Operator.

MRS. STEVENSON. *Please!*

(*Sound of ringing.*)

CHIEF OPERATOR (*coolly and professionally*). This is the Chief Operator.

MRS. STEVENSON. Chief Operator? I want you to trace a call. A telephone call. Immediately. I don't know where it came from, or who was making it, but it's absolutely necessary that it be tracked down. Because it was about a murder. Yes, a terrible, cold-blooded murder of a poor innocent woman—tonight—at eleven fifteen.

CHIEF OPERATOR. I see.

MRS. STEVENSON (*high-strung, demanding*). Can you trace it for me? Can you track down those men?

CHIEF OPERATOR. It depends, madam.

MRS. STEVENSON. Depends on what?

CHIEF OPERATOR. It depends on whether the call is still going on. If it's a live call, we can trace it on the equipment. If it's been disconnected, we can't.

MRS. STEVENSON. Disconnected?

CHIEF OPERATOR. If the parties have stopped talking to each other.

MRS. STEVENSON. Oh—but—but of course they must have stopped talking to each other by *now*. That was at least five minutes ago—and they didn't sound like the type who would make a long call.

CHIEF OPERATOR. Well, I can try tracing it. Now—what is your name, madam?

MRS. STEVENSON. Mrs. Stevenson. Mrs. Elbert Stevenson. But—listen—

CHIEF OPERATOR *(writing it down)*. And your telephone number?

MRS. STEVENSON *(more irritated)*. Plaza 3-2098. But if you go on wasting all this time—

CHIEF OPERATOR. And what is your reason for wanting this call traced?

MRS. STEVENSON. My reason? Well—for heaven's sake—isn't it obvious? I overhear two men—they're killers—they're planning to murder this woman—it's a matter for the police.

CHIEF OPERATOR. Have you told the police?

MRS. STEVENSON. No. How could I?

CHIEF OPERATOR. You're making this check into a private call purely as a private individual?

MRS. STEVENSON. Yes. But meanwhile—

CHIEF OPERATOR. Well, Mrs. Stevenson—I seriously doubt whether we could make this check for you at this time just on your say-so as a private individual. We'd have to have something more official.

MRS. STEVENSON. Oh, for heaven's sake! You mean to tell me I can't report a murder without getting tied up in all this red tape? Why, it's perfectly idiotic. All right, then. I *will* call the police. *(She slams down receiver.)* Ridiculous!
(Sound of dialing.)

SECOND OPERATOR. Your call, please?

MRS. STEVENSON *(very annoyed)*. The Police Department—*please.*

SECOND OPERATOR. Ringing the Police Department.
(*Rings twice. Phone is picked up.*)
SERGEANT DUFFY. Police Department. Precinct 43. Duffy
speaking.
MRS. STEVENSON. Police Department? Oh. This is Mrs. Stevenson
—Mrs. Elbert Smythe Stevenson of 53 North Sutton Place.
I'm calling up to report a murder.
DUFFY. Eh?
MRS. STEVENSON. I mean—the murder hasn't been committed
yet. I just overheard plans for it over the telephone . . . over
a wrong number that the operator gave me. I've been trying
to trace down the call myself, but everybody is so stupid—
and I guess in the end you're the only people who could *do*
anything.
DUFFY (*not too impressed*). Yes, ma'am.
MRS. STEVENSON (*trying to impress him*). It was a perfectly
definite murder. I heard their plans distinctly. Two men
were talking, and they were going to murder some woman
at eleven fifteen tonight—she lived in a house near a bridge.
DUFFY. Yes, ma'am.
MRS. STEVENSON. And there was a private patrolman on the
street. He was going to go around for a beer on Second
Avenue. And there was some third man—a client—who was
paying to have this poor woman murdered— They were
going to take her rings and bracelets—and use a knife—
Well, it's unnerved me dreadfully—and I'm not well—
DUFFY. I see. When was all this, ma'am?
MRS. STEVENSON. About eight minutes ago. Oh . . . (*Relieved.*)
then you *can* do something? You *do* understand—
DUFFY. And what is your name, ma'am?
MRS. STEVENSON (*impatiently*). Mrs. Stevenson. Mrs. Elbert
Stevenson.
DUFFY. And your address?
MRS. STEVENSON. 53 North Sutton Place. That's near a bridge,

the Queensborough Bridge, you know—and *we* have a private patrolman on *our* street—and Second Avenue—

DUFFY. And what was that number you were calling?

MRS. STEVENSON. Murray Hill 4-0098. But—that wasn't the number I overheard. I mean Murray Hill 4-0098 is my husband's office. He's working late tonight, and I was trying to reach him to ask him to come home. I'm an invalid, you know—and it's the maid's night off—and I *hate* to be alone —even though he says I'm perfectly safe as long as I have the telephone right beside my bed.

DUFFY (*stolidly*). Well, we'll look into it, Mrs. Stevenson, and see if we can check it with the telephone company.

MRS. STEVENSON (*getting impatient*). But the telephone company said they couldn't check the call if the parties had stopped talking. I've already taken care of *that*.

DUFFY. Oh, yes?

MRS. STEVENSON (*highhanded*). Personally I feel you ought to do something far more immediate and drastic than just check the call. What good does checking the call do, if they've stopped talking? By the time you track it down, they'll already have committed the murder.

DUFFY. Well, we'll take care of it, lady. Don't worry.

MRS. STEVENSON. I'd say the whole thing calls for a search—a complete and thorough search of the whole city. I'm very near a bridge, and I'm not far from Second Avenue. And I know *I'd* feel a whole lot better if you sent around a radio car to *this* neighborhood at once.

DUFFY. And what makes you think the murder's going to be committed in your neighborhood, ma'am?

MRS. STEVENSON. Oh, I don't know. The coincidence is so horrible. Second Avenue—the patrolman—the bridge—

DUFFY. Second Avenue is a very long street, ma'am. And do you happen to know how many bridges there are in the city of New York alone? Not to mention Brooklyn, Staten

Island, Queens, and the Bronx? And how do you know there isn't some little house out on Staten Island—on some little Second Avenue you've never heard about? How do you know they were even talking about New York at all?

MRS. STEVENSON. But I heard the call on the New York dialing system.

DUFFY. How do you know it wasn't a long-distance call you overheard? Telephones are funny things. Look, lady, why don't you look at it this way? Supposing you hadn't broken in on that telephone call? Supposing you'd got your husband the way you always do? Would this murder have made any difference to you then?

MRS. STEVENSON. I suppose not. But it's so inhuman—so cold-blooded—

DUFFY. A lot of murders are committed in this city every day, ma'am. If we could do something to stop 'em, we would. But a clue of this kind that's so vague isn't much more use to us than no clue at all.

MRS. STEVENSON. But surely—

DUFFY. Unless, of course, you have some reason for thinking this call is phony—and that someone may be planning to murder *you?*

MRS. STEVENSON. *Me?* Oh, no, I hardly think so. I—I mean—why should anybody? I'm alone all day and night—I see nobody except my maid Eloise—she's a big two-hundred-pounder—she's too lazy to bring up my breakfast tray—and the only other person is my husband Elbert—he's crazy about me—adores me—waits on me hand and foot—he's scarcely left my side since I took sick twelve years ago—

DUFFY. Well, then, there's nothing for you to worry about, is there? And now, if you'll just leave the rest of this to us—

MRS. STEVENSON. But what will you *do?* It's so late—it's nearly eleven o'clock.

DUFFY (*firmly*). We'll take care of it, lady.

MRS. STEVENSON. Will you broadcast it all over the city? And send out squads? And warn your radio cars to watch out—especially in suspicious neighborhoods like mine?

DUFFY (*more firmly*). Lady, I *said* we'd take care of it. Just now I've got a couple of other matters here on my desk that require my immediate—

MRS. STEVENSON. Oh! (*She slams down receiver hard.*) Idiot. (*Looking at phone nervously.*) Now, why did I do that? Now he'll think I *am* a fool. Oh, why doesn't Elbert come home? *Why* doesn't he?

(*Sound of dialing* OPERATOR.)

OPERATOR. Your call, please?

MRS. STEVENSON. Operator, for heaven's sake, will you ring that Murray Hill 4-0098 number again? I can't think what's keeping him so long.

OPERATOR. Ringing Murray Hill 4-0098. (*Dials. Busy signal.*) The line is busy. Shall I—

MRS. STEVENSON (*nastily*). I can hear it. You don't have to tell me. I know it's busy. (*Slams down receiver.*) If I could only get out of this bed for a little while. If I could get a breath of fresh air—or just lean out the window—and see the street— (*The phone rings. She darts for it instantly.*) Hello. Elbert? Hello. Hello. Hello. Oh, what's the *matter* with this phone? *Hello? Hello?* (*Slams down receiver. The phone rings again, once. She picks it up.*) Hello? Hello—Oh, for heaven's sake, who *is* this? Hello, hello. *Hello.* (*Slams down receiver. Dials* OPERATOR.)

THIRD OPERATOR. Your call, please?

MRS. STEVENSON (*very annoyed and imperious*). Hello, operator. I don't know what's the matter with this telephone tonight, but it's positively driving me crazy. I've never seen such inefficient, miserable service. Now, look. I'm an invalid, and I'm very nervous, and I'm *not* supposed to be annoyed. But if this keeps on much longer—

THIRD OPERATOR (*a young, sweet type*). What seems to be the trouble, madam?

MRS. STEVENSON. Well, everything's wrong. The whole world could be murdered, for all you people care. And now, my phone keeps ringing—

OPERATOR. Yes, madam?

MRS. STEVENSON. Ringing and ringing and ringing every five seconds or so, and when I pick it up, there's no one there.

OPERATOR. I am sorry, madam. If you will hang up, I will test it for you.

MRS. STEVENSON. I don't want you to test it for me. I want you to put through that call—whatever it is—at once.

OPERATOR (*gently*). I am afraid that is not possible, madam.

MRS. STEVENSON (*storming*). Not possible? And why, may I ask?

OPERATOR. The system is automatic, madam. If someone is trying to dial your number, there is no way to check whether the call is coming through the system or not— unless the person who is trying to reach you complains to his particular operator.

MRS. STEVENSON. Well, of all the stupid, complicated—! And meanwhile *I've* got to sit here in my bed, *suffering* every time that phone rings, imagining everything—

OPERATOR. I will try to check it for you, madam.

MRS. STEVENSON. Check it! Check it! That's all anybody can do. Of all the stupid, idiotic . . . ! (*She hangs up.*) Oh—what's the use . . . (*Instantly* MRS. STEVENSON's *phone rings again. She picks up the receiver. Wildly.*) Hello. HELLO. Stop ringing, do you hear me? Answer me? What do you want? Do you realize you're driving me crazy? Stark, staring—

MAN (*dull, flat voice*). Hello. Is this Plaza 3-2098?

MRS. STEVENSON (*catching her breath*). Yes. Yes. This is Plaza 3-2098.

MAN. This is Western Union. I have a telegram here for Mrs. Elbert Stevenson. Is there anyone there to receive the message?

MRS. STEVENSON (*trying to calm herself*). I am Mrs. Stevenson.

WESTERN UNION (*reading flatly*). The telegram is as follows: "Mrs. Elbert Stevenson. 53 North Sutton Place, New York, New York. Darling. Terribly sorry. Tried to get you for last hour, but line busy. Leaving for Boston 11 P.M. tonight on urgent business. Back tomorrow afternoon. Keep happy. Love. Signed. Elbert."

MRS. STEVENSON (*breathlessly, aghast, to herself*). Oh—no—

WESTERN UNION. That is all, madam. Do you wish us to deliver a copy of the message?

MRS. STEVENSON. No—no, thank you.

WESTERN UNION MAN. Thank you, madam. Good night. (*He hangs up phone.*)

MRS. STEVENSON (*mechanically, to phone*). Good night. (*She hangs up slowly, suddenly bursting into tears.*) No—no—it isn't true! He couldn't do it. Not when he knows I'll be all alone. It's some trick—some fiendish— (*She dials* OPERATOR.)

OPERATOR (*coolly*). Your call, please?

MRS. STEVENSON. Operator—try that Murray Hill 4-0098 number for me just once more, please.

OPERATOR. Ringing Murray Hill 4-0098. (*Call goes through. We hear ringing at other end. Ring after ring.*)

MRS. STEVENSON. He's gone. Oh, Elbert, how could you? How could you—? (*She hangs up phone, sobbing pityingly to herself, turning restlessly.*) But I can't be alone tonight. I can't. If I'm alone one more second— I don't care what he says—or what the expense is—I'm a sick woman—I'm entitled— (*She dials* INFORMATION.)

INFORMATION. This is Information.

MRS. STEVENSON. I want the telephone number of Henchley Hospital.

INFORMATION. Henchley Hospital? Do you have the address, madam?

MRS. STEVENSON. No. It's somewhere in the seventies, though. It's a very small, private, and exclusive hospital where I had my appendix out two years ago. Henchley. H-E-N-C—

INFORMATION. One moment, please.

MRS. STEVENSON. Please—hurry. And please—what *is* the time?

INFORMATION. I do not know, madam. You may find out the time by dialing Meridian 7-1212.

MRS. STEVENSON *(irritated)*. Oh, for heaven's sake! Couldn't you—?

INFORMATION. The number of Henchley Hospital is Butterfield 8-1598, madam.

MRS. STEVENSON. Butterfield 8-1598. *(She hangs up before she finishes speaking, and immediately dials number as she repeats it.)*
(Phone rings.)

WOMAN *(middle-aged, solid, firm, practical)*. Henchley Hospital, good evening.

MRS. STEVENSON. Nurses' Registry.

WOMAN. Who was it you wished to speak to, please?

MRS. STEVENSON *(highhanded)*. I want the Nurses' Registry at once. I want a trained nurse. I want to hire her immediately. For the night.

WOMAN. I see. And what is the nature of the case, Madam?

MRS. STEVENSON. Nerves. I'm very nervous. I need soothing— a. ' companionship. My husband is away—and I'm—

WOMAN. Have you been recommended to us by any doctor in particular, madam?

MRS. STEVENSON. No. But I really don't see why all this cate- chizing is necessary. I want a trained nurse. I was a patient in your hospital two years ago. And after all, I *do* expect to *pay* this person—

WOMAN. We quite understand that, madam. But registered nurses are very scarce just now—and our superintendent has asked us to send people out only on cases where the physician in charge feels it is absolutely necessary.

MRS. STEVENSON (*growing hysterical*). Well, it *is* absolutely necessary. I'm a sick woman. I—I'm very upset. Very. I'm alone in this house—and I'm an invalid—and tonight I overheard a telephone conversation that upset me dreadfully. About a murder—a poor woman who was going to be murdered at eleven fifteen tonight—in fact, if someone doesn't come at once—I'm afraid I'll go out of my mind— (*Almost off handle by now.*)

WOMAN (*calmly*). I see. Well, I'll speak to Miss Phillips as soon as she comes in. And what is your name, madam?

MRS. STEVENSON. Miss Phillips. And when do you expect her in?

WOMAN. I really don't know, madam. She went out to supper at eleven o'clock.

MRS. STEVENSON. Eleven o'clock. But it's not eleven yet. (*She cries out.*) Oh, my clock *has* stopped. I thought it was running down. What time is it?

WOMAN. Just fourteen minutes past eleven.

(*Sound of phone receiver being lifted on same line as* MRS. STEVENSON'S. *A click.*)

MRS. STEVENSON (*crying out*). What's *that?*

WOMAN. What was what, madam?

MRS. STEVENSON. That—that click just now—in my own telephone? As though someone had lifted the receiver off the hook of the extension phone downstairs—

WOMAN. I didn't hear it, madam. Now—about this—

MRS. STEVENSON (*scared*). But I *did*. There's someone in this house. Someone downstairs in the kitchen. And they're listening to me now. They're—*(Hangs up phone. In a suffocated voice.)* I won't pick it up. I won't let them hear me. I'll be quiet—and they'll think— *(With growing terror.)* But if I don't call someone now—while they're still down there—there'll be no time. *(She picks up receiver. Bland buzzing signal. She dials* OPERATOR. *Rings twice.)*

OPERATOR *(fat and lethargic)*. Your call, please?

MRS. STEVENSON *(a desperate whisper)*. Operator, I—I'm in desperate trouble—I—

OPERATOR. I cannot hear you, madam. Please speak louder.

MRS. STEVENSON *(still whispering)*. I don't dare. I—there's someone listening. Can you hear me now?

OPERATOR. Your call, please? What number are you calling, madam?

MRS. STEVENSON *(desperately)*. You've got to hear me. Oh, please. You've got to help me. There's someone in this house. Someone who's going to murder me. And you've got to get in touch with the— *(Click of receiver being put down in* MRS. STEVENSON*'s line. Bursting out wildly.)* Oh, there it is—he's put it down—he's put down the extension— he's coming— *(She screams.)* He's coming up the stairs— *(Hoarsely.)* Give me the Police Department— *(Screaming.)* The police!

OPERATOR. Ringing the Police Department.

(Phone is rung. We hear sound of a train beginning to fade in. On second ring, MRS. STEVENSON *screams again, but roaring of train drowns out her voice. For a few seconds we hear nothing but roaring of train, then dying away, phone at police headquarters ringing.)*

DUFFY Police Department. Precinct 43. Duffy speaking. *(Pause.)* Police Department. Duffy speaking.

GEORGE. Sorry. Wrong number. *(Hangs up.)*

FOR DISCUSSION

1. Who hires the killers to murder Mrs. Stevenson? What are his motives?

2. What are the most important facts we learn about the killers when Mrs. Stevenson overhears their conversation?

3. *Sorry, Wrong Number* is a suspense play. As you read the play, did you feel that you had more insight into what was happening than Mrs. Stevenson did? What things make the feeling of excitement build up?

4. Our natural tendency is to feel pity for a woman who is confined to bed. What feeling do you have toward Mrs. Stevenson?

5. Try reading Mrs. Stevenson's first five or six lines to the rest of the class. What qualities in Mrs. Stevenson's personality are shown in these lines? Can the *way* you read the lines cause the class to dislike her? Is there any danger of disliking her too much? What might happen to the audience if they really hated her?

6. Why do you think the author tells us what kind of person Mrs. Stevenson is so early in the play?

7. What was the main reason that Mrs. Stevenson was unable to protect her own life, even though she overheard the killers on the telephone?

8. Sometimes we can see a color more clearly if we use it with a contrasting color. In a play, we are able to understand a character better if he is contrasted with another character. You may have noticed the contrast between Mrs. Stevenson and the telephone operator. In what ways are they different? Do any other characters contrast with Mrs. Stevenson?

9. Have you ever figured out the ending of a suspense program on television because you looked at the clock and discovered that the program had only five minutes of running time left? Sometimes if you know *when* the ending will occur, you have a pretty good idea of *what* the ending will be. Only certain things can happen in that amount of time. In *Sorry, Wrong Number* we are told near the beginning of the play that the murder will be committed at 11:15 p.m.

We are then given a false clue as to what time it actually is. What is the false clue? When is the first time that we know exactly how close it is to 11:15? Why do you suppose the author planted a false clue?

10. The setting for this play is New York City. What elements of big city life does the author use in her play? The play actually could have taken place in other large cities, but many changes would have been needed if the action had taken place in a smaller community. What changes would be necessary?

FOR COMPOSITION

1. Could Mrs. Stevenson have prevented the crime? Write a paragraph in which you tell why Mrs. Stevenson could or could not have stopped the crime from happening.

2. What kind of man is Elbert Stevenson? What should he look like? Can you imagine his personality as well as his appearance? Write a twelve- to fifteen-line description of Mr. Stevenson.

A SPECIAL ACTIVITY

You are the adjustment manager in a department store. Mrs. Stevenson calls because the lamp that was sent out to her has the wrong color lampshade. Lampshades of the right color are out of stock. She is angry and demands a refund. You want to persuade her to exchange the lamp for another one because it is the policy of the store to make exchanges instead of refunds whenever possible. It is also the policy of the store that "the customer is always right." Act out a telephone conversation between Mrs. Stevenson and the adjustment manager, making up lines as you go along. Remember that Mrs. Stevenson's personality should be the same as it is in *Sorry, Wrong Number*. One other point: the store insists that this kind of telephone call last no longer than five minutes.

THE JEWELS
OF THE SHRINE

JAMES ENE HENSHAW

THE JEWELS OF THE SHRINE

Almost everyone likes to be treated with dignity and respect.

Okorie, the old man who is the main character in *The Jewels of the Shrine*, believes that this kind of treatment is due him simply because he is old and because he lives in a society where elders are respected. His grandsons, however, see treating the old with respect as an old-fashioned custom, which is out of tune with their times.

In reading this play, which takes place in an economically undeveloped part of Africa, notice how the characters on both sides of the generation gap show their basic feelings of pride, greed, vengefulness, and distrust.

CHARACTERS

OKORIE, an old man

AROB and OJIMA, OKORIE's grandsons

BASSI, a woman

A STRANGER

(Scene: An imaginary village close to a town in Nigeria. All the scenes of this play take place in OKORIE's *mud-walled house. The time is the present.)*

SCENE I

(The hall in OKORIE's *house. There are three doors. One leads directly into* OKORIE's *room. The two others are on either side of the hall. Of these, one leads to his grandsons' apartment, whilst the other acts as a general exit.)*
(The chief items of furniture consist of a wide bamboo bed, on which is spread a mat; a wooden chair, a low table, and a few odds and ends, including three hoes.)
*(*OKORIE, *an old man of about eighty years of age, with scanty grey hair, and dressed in the way his village folk do, is sitting at the edge of the bed. He holds a stout, rough walking-stick and a horn filled with palm wine.)*

(On the wooden chair near the bed sits a STRANGER, *a man of about forty-five years of age. He, too, occasionally sips wine from a calabash cup. It is evening. The room is rather dark, and a cloth-in-oil lantern hangs from a hook on the wall.)*

OKORIE. Believe me, Stranger, in my days things were different. It was a happy thing to become an old man, because young people were taught to respect elderly men.

STRANGER *(sipping his wine)*. Here in the village you should be happier. In the town where I come from, a boy of ten riding a hired bicycle will knock down a man of fifty years without any feeling of pity.

OKORIE. Bicycle. That is why I have not been to town for ten years. Town people seem to enjoy rushing about doing nothing. It kills them.

STRANGER. You are lucky that you have your grandchildren to help you. Many people in town have no one to help them.

OKORIE. Look at me, Stranger, and tell me if these shabby clothes and this dirty beard show that I have good grandchildren. Believe me, Stranger, in my younger days things were different. Old men were happy. When they died, they were buried with honor. But in my case, Stranger, my old age has been unhappy. And my only fear now is that when I die, my grandsons will not accord me the honor due to my age. It will be a disgrace to me.

STRANGER. I will now go on my way, Okorie. May God help you.

OKORIE. I need help, Stranger, for although I have two grandsons, I am lonely and unhappy because they do not love or care for me. They tell me that I am from an older world. Farewell, Stranger. If you call again and I am alive, I will welcome you back. *(Exit* STRANGER. BASSI, *a beautiful woman of about thirty years, enters.)*

BASSI. Who was that man, Grandfather?

OKORIE. He was a stranger.

BASSI. I do not trust strangers. They may appear honest when the lights are on. But as soon as there is darkness, they creep back as thieves. [OKORIE *smiles and drinks his wine.* BASSI *points to him.*] What has happened, Grandfather? When I left you this afternoon, you were old, your mind was worried, and your eyes were swollen. Where now are the care, the sorrow, the tears in your eyes? You never smiled before, but now—

OKORIE. The stranger has brought happiness back into my life. He has given me hope again.

BASSI. But don't they preach in town that it is only God who gives hope? Every other thing gives despair.

OKORIE. Perhaps that stranger was God. Don't the preachers say that God moves like a stranger?

BASSI. God moves in strange ways.

OKORIE. Yes, I believe it, because since that stranger came, I have felt younger again. You know, woman, when I worshipped at our forefathers' shrine, I was happy. I knew what it was all about. It was my life. Then the preachers came, and I abandoned the beliefs of our fathers. The old ways did not leave me; the new ways did not wholly accept me. I was therefore unhappy. But soon I felt the wings of God carrying me high. And with my loving and helpful son, I thought that my old age would be as happy as that of my father before me. But death played me a trick. My son died and I was left to the mercy of his two sons. Once more unhappiness gripped my life. With all their education my grandsons lacked one thing—respect for age. But today the stranger who came here has once more brought happiness to me. Let me tell you this—

BASSI. It is enough, Grandfather. Long talks make you tired. Come, your food is now ready.

OKORIE *(happily).* Woman, I cannot eat. When happiness fills your heart, you cannot eat. *(Two voices are heard outside, laughing and swearing.)*

BASSI. Your grandchildren are coming back.

OKORIE. Don't call them my grandchildren. I am alone in this world. (*Door flings open. Two young men, about eighteen and twenty, enter the room. They are in shirt and trousers.*)

AROB. By our forefathers, Grandfather, you are still awake!

BASSI. Why should he not keep awake if he likes?

AROB. But Grandfather usually goes to bed before the earliest chicken thinks of it.

OJIMA. Our good grandfather might be thinking of his youthful days, when all young men were fond of farming and all young women loved the kitchen.

BASSI. Shame on both of you for talking to an old man like that. When you grow old, your own children will laugh and jeer at you. Come, Grandfather, and take your food. (OKORIE *stands up with difficulty and limps with the aid of his stick through the exit, followed by* BASSI, *who casts a reproachful look on the two men before she leaves.*)

AROB. I wonder what Grandfather and the woman were talking about.

OJIMA. It must be the usual thing. We are bad boys. We have no regard for the memory of our father, and so on.

AROB. Our father left his responsibility to us. Nature had arranged that he should bury Grandfather before thinking of himself.

OJIMA. But would Grandfather listen to Nature when it comes to the matter of death? Everybody in his generation, including all his wives, have died. But Grandfather has made a bet with death. And it seems that he will win.

OKORIE (*calling from offstage*). Bassi! Bassi! Where is that woman?

OJIMA. The old man is coming. Let us hide ourselves. (*Both rush under the bed.*)

OKORIE (*comes in, limping on his stick as usual*). Bassi, where are you? Haven't I told that girl never—

BASSI (*entering*). Don't shout so. It's not good for you.

OKORIE. Where are the two people?

BASSI. You mean your grandsons?

OKORIE. My, my, well, call them what you like.

BASSI. They are not here. They must have gone into their room.

OKORIE. Bassi, I have a secret for you. *(He narrows his eyes.)* A big secret. *(His hands tremble.)* Can you keep a secret?

BASSI. Of course I can.

OKORIE *(rubbing his forehead)*. You can, what can you? What did I say?

BASSI *(holding him and leading him to sit on the bed)*. You are excited. You know that whenever you are excited, you begin to forget things.

OKORIE. That is not my fault. It is old age. Well, but what was I saying?

BASSI. You asked me if I could keep a secret.

OKORIE. Yes, yes, a great secret. You know, Bassi, I have been an unhappy man.

BASSI. I have heard it all before.

OKORIE. Listen, woman. My dear son died and left me to the mercy of his two sons. They are the worst grandsons in the land. They have sold all that their father left. They do not care for me. Now when I die, what will they do to me? Don't you think that they will abandon me in disgrace? An old man has a right to be properly cared for. And when he dies, he has a right to a good burial. But my grandchildren do not think of these things.

BASSI. See how you tremble, Grandfather! I have told you not to think of such things.

OKORIE. Why should I not? But sh! . . . I hear a voice.

BASSI. It's only your ears deceiving you, Grandfather.

OKORIE. It is not my ears, woman. I know when old age hums in my ears and tired nerves ring bells in my head, but I know also when I hear a human voice.

BASSI. Go on, Grandfather; there is no one.

OKORIE. Now, listen. You saw the stranger that came here. He gave me hope. But wait, look around, Bassi. Make sure that no one is listening to us.

BASSI. No one, Grandfather.

OKORIE. Open the door and look.

BASSI (*opens the exit door*). No one.

OKORIE. Look into that corner.

BASSI (*looks*). There is no one.

OKORIE. Look under the bed.

BASSI (*irritably*). I won't, Grandfather. There is no need; I have told you that there is nobody in the house.

OKORIE (*pitiably*). I have forgotten what I was talking about.

BASSI (*calmly*). You have a secret from the stranger.

OKORIE. Yes, the stranger told me something. Have you ever heard of the "Jewels of the Shrine"?

BASSI. Real jewels?

OKORIE. Yes. Among the beads which my father got from the early white men, were real jewels. When war broke out and a great fever invaded all our lands, my father made a sacrifice in the village shrine. He promised that if this village were spared, he would offer his costly jewels to the shrine. Death roamed through all the other villages, but not one person in this village died of the fever. My father kept his promise. In a big ceremony the jewels were placed on our shrine. But it was not for long. Some said they were stolen. But the stranger who came here knew where they were. He said that they were buried somewhere near the big oak tree on our farm. I must go out and dig for them. They can be sold for fifty pounds these days.

BASSI. But, Grandfather, it will kill you to go out in this cold and darkness. You must get someone to do it for you. You cannot lift a hoe.

OKORIE (*infuriated*). So, you believe I am too old to lift a hoe. You, you, oh, I . . .

BASSI *(coaxing him)*. There now, young man, no temper. If you wish, I myself will dig up the whole farm for you.

OKORIE. Every bit of it?

BASSI. Yes.

OKORIE. And hand over to me all that you will find?

BASSI. Yes.

OKORIE. And you will not tell my grandsons?

BASSI. No, Grandfather, I will not.

OKORIE. Swear, woman, swear by our fathers' shrine.

BASSI. I swear.

OKORIE *(relaxing)*. Now life is becoming worthwhile. Tell no one about it, woman. Begin digging tomorrow morning. Dig inch by inch until you bring out the jewels of our forefathers' shrine.

BASSI. I am tired, Grandfather. I must sleep now. Good night.

OKORIE *(with feeling)*. Good night. God and our fathers' spirits keep you. When dangerous bats alight on the roofs of wicked men, let them not trouble you in your sleep. When far-seeing owls hoot the menace of future days, let their evil prophecies keep off your path. (BASSI *leaves.* OKORIE, *standing up and trembling, moves to a corner and brings out a small hoe. Struggling with his senile joints, he tries to imitate a young man digging.*)

Oh, who said I was old? After all, I am only eighty years. And I feel younger than most young men. Let me see how I can dig. *(He tries to dig again.)* Ah! I feel aches all over my hip. Maybe the soil here is too hard. *(He listens.)* How I keep on thinking that I hear people whispering in this room! I must rest now. *(Carrying the hoe with him, he goes in to his room.* AROB *and* OJIMA *crawl out from under the bed.)*

AROB *(stretching his hip)*. My hip, oh my hip!

OJIMA. My legs!

AROB. So there is a treasure in our farm! We must waste no time; we must begin digging soon.

OJIMA. Soon? We must begin tonight—now. The old man has taken one hoe. *(Pointing to the corner.)* There are two over there. *(They fetch two hoes from among the heap of things in a corner of the room.)* If we can only get the jewels, we can go and live in town and let the old man manage as he can. Let's move now. *(As they are about to go out, each holding a hoe, OKORIE comes out with his own hoe. For a moment the three stare at each other in silence and surprise.)*

AROB. Now, Grandfather, where are you going with a hoe at this time of night?

OJIMA *(impudently)*. Yes, Grandfather, what is the idea?

OKORIE. I should ask you; this is my house. Why are you creeping about like thieves?

AROB. All right, Grandfather, we are going back to bed.

OKORIE. What are you doing with hoes? You were never fond of farming.

OJIMA. We intend to go to the farm early in the morning.

OKORIE. But the harvest is over. When everybody in the village was digging out the crops, you were going around the town with your hands in your pockets. Now you say you are going to the farm.

OJIMA. Digging is good for the health, Grandfather.

OKORIE *(re-entering his room)*. Good night.

AROB *and* OJIMA. Good night, Grandfather.

(They return to their room. After a short time AROB and OJIMA come out, each holding a hoe, and tiptoe out through the exit. Then, gently, OKORIE too comes out on his toes, and placing the hoe on his shoulder, warily leaves the hall.)

Curtain.

SCENE II

(The same, the following morning.)

BASSI *(knocking at* OKORIE'S *door; she is holding a hoe).* Grandfather, wake up. I am going to the farm.

OKORIE *(opening the door).* Good morning. Where are you going so early in the morning?

BASSI. I am going to dig up the farm. You remember the treasure, don't you?

OKORIE. Do you expect to find a treasure whilst you sleep at night? You should have dug at night, woman. Treasures are never found in the day.

BASSI. But you told me to dig in the morning, Grandfather.

OKORIE. My grandsons were in this room somewhere. They heard what I told you about the Jewels of the Shrine.

BASSI. They could not have heard us. I looked everywhere. The stranger must have told them.

OKORIE *(rubbing his forehead).* What stranger?

BASSI. The stranger who told you about the treasure in the farm.

OKORIE. So it was a stranger who told me! Oh, yes, a stranger! *(He begins to dream.)* Ah, I remember him now. He was a great man. His face shone like the sun. It was like the face of God.

BASSI. You are dreaming, Grandfather. Wake up! I must go to the farm quickly.

OKORIE. Yes, woman, I remember the jewels in the farm. But you are too late.

BASSI *(excitedly).* Late? Have your grandsons discovered the treasure?

OKORIE. They have not, but I have discovered it myself.

BASSI *(amazed).* You? *(*OKORIE *nods his head with a smile on his face.)* Do you mean to say that you are now a rich man?

OKORIE. By our fathers' shrine, I am.

BASSI. So you went and worked at night. You should not have done it, even to forestall your grandchildren.

OKORIE. My grandsons would never have found it.

BASSI. But you said that they heard us talking of the treasure.

OKORIE. You see, I suspected that my grandsons were in this room. So I told you that the treasure was in the farm, but in actual fact it was in the little garden behind this house, where the village shrine used to be. My grandsons travelled half a mile to the farm last night for nothing.

BASSI. Then I am glad I did not waste my time.

OKORIE (*with delight*). How my grandsons must have toiled in the night! (*He is overcome with laughter.*) My grandsons, they thought I would die in disgrace, a pauper, unheard of. No, not now. (*Then boldly.*) But those wicked children must change, or when I die, I shall not leave a penny for them.

BASSI. Oh, Grandfather, to think you are a rich man!

OKORIE. I shall send you to buy me new clothes. My grandsons will not know me again. Ha—ha—ha—ha! (OKORIE *and* BASSI *leave.* AROB *and* OJIMA *crawl out from under the bed, where for a second time they have hidden. They look rough, their feet dirty with sand and leaves. Each comes out with his hoe.*)

AROB. So the old man fooled us.

OJIMA. Well, he is now a rich man, and we must treat him with care.

AROB. We have no choice. He says that unless we change, he will not leave a penny to us.

A knock at the door.

AROB *and* OJIMA. Come in.

OKORIE (*comes in, and seeing them so rough and dirty, bursts out laughing; the others look surprised*). Look how dirty you are, with hoes and all. "Gentlemen" like you should not touch hoes. You should wear white gloves and live in towns. But see, you look like two pigs. Ha—ha—ha—ha—ha! Oh what grandsons! How stupid they look! Ha—ha—ha! (AROB *and* OJIMA *are dumbfounded.*) I saw both of you a short while ago under the bed. I hope you now know that I have got the Jewels of the Shrine.

AROB. We, too, have something to tell you, Grandfather.

OKORIE. Yes, yes, "gentlemen." Come, tell me. (*He begins to move away.*) You must hurry up. I am going to town to buy myself some new clothes and a pair of shoes.

AROB. New clothes?

OJIMA. And shoes?

OKORIE. Yes, grandsons, it is never too late to wear new clothes.

AROB. Let us go and buy them for you. It is too hard for you to—

OKORIE. If God does not think that I am yet old enough to be in the grave, I do not think I am too old to go to the market in town. I need some clothes and a comb to comb my beard. I am happy, grandchildren, very happy. (AROB *and* OJIMA *are dumbfounded.*) Now, "gentlemen," why don't you get drunk and shout at me as before? (*Growing bolder.*) Why not laugh at me as if I were nobody? You young puppies, I am now somebody, somebody. What is somebody? (*Rubbing his forehead as usual.*)

AROB (*to* OJIMA). He has forgotten again.

OKORIE. Who has forgotten what?

OJIMA. You have forgotten nothing. You are a good man, Grandfather, and we like you.

OKORIE (*shouting excitedly*). Bassi! Bassi! Bassi! Where is that silly woman? Bassi, come and hear this. My grandchildren like me; I am now a good man. Ha—ha—ha—ha! (*He limps into his room.* AROB *and* OJIMA *look at each other. It is obvious to them that the old man has all the cards now.*)

AROB. What has come over the old man?

OJIMA. Have you not heard that when people have money, it scratches them on the brain? That is what has happened to our grandfather now.

AROB. He does not believe that we like him. How can we convince him?

OJIMA. You know what he likes most: someone to scratch his back. When he comes out, you will scratch his back, and I will use his big fan to fan at him.

AROB. Great idea. (OKORIE *coughs from the room.*) He is coming now.

OKORIE *(comes in).* I am so tired.

AROB. You said you were going to the market, Grandfather.

OKORIE. You do well to remind me. I have sent Bassi to buy the things I want.

OJIMA. Grandfather, you look really tired. Lie down here. (OKORIE *lies down and uncovers his back.*) Grandfather, from now on, I shall give you all your breakfast and your midday meals.

AROB *(jealously).* By our forefathers' shrine, Grandfather, I shall take care of your dinner and supply you with wine and clothing.

OKORIE. God bless you, little sons. That is how it should have been all the time. An old man has a right to live comfortably in his last days.

OJIMA. Grandfather, it is a very long time since we scratched your back.

AROB. Yes, it is a long time. We have not done it since we were infants. We want to do it now. It will remind us of our younger days, when it was a pleasure to scratch your back.

OKORIE. Scratch my back? Ha—ha—ha—ha. Oh, go on, go on; by our fathers' shrine you are now good men. I wonder what has happened to you.

OJIMA. It's you, Grandfather. You are such a nice man. As a younger man you must have looked very well. But in your old age you look simply wonderful.

AROB. That is right, Grandfather, and let us tell you again. Do not waste a penny of yours any more. We will keep you happy and satisfied to the last hour of your life. (*OKORIE appears pleased.* AROB *now begins to pick at, and scratch,* OKORIE's *back.* OJIMA *kneels near the bed and begins to fan the old man. After a while a slow snore is heard. Then, as* AROB *warms up to his task,* OKORIE *jumps up.*)

OKORIE. Oh, that one hurts. Gently, children, gently. (*He relaxes and soon begins to snore again.* OJIMA *and* AROB *gradually stand up.*)

AROB. The old fogy is asleep.

OJIMA. That was clever of us. I am sure he believes us now. (*They leave.* OKORIE *opens an eye and peeps at them. Then he smiles and closes it again.* BASSI *enters, bringing some new clothes, a pair of shoes, a comb and brush, a tin of face powder, etc. She pushes* OKORIE.)

BASSI. Wake up, Grandfather.

OKORIE (*opening his eyes*). Who told you that I was asleep? Oh! you have brought the things. It is so long since I had a change of clothes. Go on, woman, and call those grandsons of mine. They must help me to put on my new clothes and shoes. (*BASSI leaves.* OKORIE *begins to comb his hair and beard, which have not been touched for a long time.* BASSI *re-enters with* AROB *and* OJIMA. *Helped by his grandsons and* BASSI, OKORIE *puts on his new clothes and shoes. He then sits on the bed and poses majestically like a chief.*)

(*Curtain.*)

SCENE III

(*The same, a few months later.* OKORIE *is lying on the bed. He is well dressed and looks happy, but it is easily seen that he is nearing his end. There is a knock at the door.* OKORIE *turns and looks at the door but cannot speak loudly. Another knock; the door opens, and the* STRANGER *enters.)*

OKORIE. Welcome back, Stranger. You have come in time. Sit down. I will tell you of my will. *(Door opens slowly.* BASSI *walks in.)*

BASSI *(to* STRANGER*).* How is he?

STRANGER. Just holding on.

BASSI. Did he say anything?

STRANGER. He says that he wants to tell me about his will. Call his grandsons. *(*BASSI *leaves.)*

OKORIE. Stranger.

STRANGER. Yes, Grandfather.

OKORIE. Do you remember what I told you about my fears in life?

STRANGER. You were afraid your last days would be miserable and that you would not have a decent burial.

OKORIE. Now, Stranger, all that is past. Don't you see how happy I am? I have been very well cared for since I saw you last. My grandchildren have done everything for me, and I am sure they will bury me with great ceremony and rejoicing. I want you to be here when I am making my will. Bend to my ears; I will whisper something to you. *(*STRANGER *bends for a moment.* OKORIE *whispers. Then he speaks aloud.)* Is that clear, Stranger?

STRANGER. It is clear.

OKORIE. Will you remember?

STRANGER. I will.

OKORIE. Do you promise?

STRANGER. I promise.

OKORIE *(relaxing on his pillow).* There now. My end will be more cheerful than I ever expected. *(A knock.)*

STRANGER. Come in. *(*AROB, OJIMA, *and* BASSI *enter. The two men appear as sad as possible. They are surprised to meet the* STRANGER, *and stare at him for a moment.)*

OKORIE (*with effort*). This man may be a stranger to you, but not to me. He is my friend. Arob, look how sad you are! Ojima, how tight your lips are with sorrow! Barely a short while ago you would not have cared whether I lived or died.

AROB. Don't speak like that, Grandfather.

OKORIE. Why should I not? Remember, these are my last words on earth.

OJIMA. You torture us, Grandfather.

OKORIE. Since my son, your father, died, you have tortured me. But now you have changed, and it is good to forgive you both.

STRANGER. You wanted to make a will.

OKORIE. Will? Yes, will. Where is Bassi? Has that woman run away already?

BASSI (*standing above the bed*). No, Grandfather, I am here.

OKORIE. Now there is my family complete.

STRANGER. The will, Grandfather, the will.

OKORIE. Oh, the will; the will is made.

AROB. Made? Where is it?

OKORIE. It is written out on paper. (AROB *and* OJIMA *together.*)

AROB. Written?

OJIMA. What?

OKORIE (*coolly*). Yes, someone wrote it for me soon after I had discovered the treasure.

AROB. Where is it, Grandfather?

OJIMA. Are you going to show us, Grandfather?

OKORIE. Yes, I will. Why not? But not now, not until I am dead.

AROB *and* OJIMA. What?

OKORIE. Listen here. The will is in a small box buried somewhere. The box also contains all my wealth. These are my wishes. Make my burial the best you can. Spend as much as is required, for you will be compensated. Do not forget that I am the oldest man in this village. An old man has a right to be decently buried. Remember, it was only after I had discovered the Jewels of the Shrine that you began to take good care of me. You should, by carrying out all my last wishes, atone for all those years when you left me poor, destitute, and miserable.

(*To the* STRANGER, *in broken phrases.*) Two weeks after my death, Stranger, you will come and unearth the box of my treasure. Open it in the presence of my grandsons. Read out the division of the property, and share it among them. Bassi, you have nothing. You have a good husband and a family. No reward or treasure is greater than a good marriage and a happy home. Stranger, I have told you where the box containing the will is buried. That is all. May God . . .

AROB *and* OJIMA (*rushing to him*). Grandfather, Grandfather—

STRANGER. Leave him in peace. (BASSI, *giving out a scream, rushes from the room.*) I must go now. Don't forget his will. Unless you bury him with great honour, you may not touch his property. (*He leaves.*)

(*Curtain.*)

SCENE IV

(*All in this scene are dressed in black.* AROB, OJIMA, *and* BASSI *are sitting around the table. There is one extra chair. The bed is still there, but the mat is taken off, leaving it bare. The hoe with which* OKORIE *dug out the treasure is lying on the bed as a sort of memorial.*)

AROB. Thank God, today is here at last. When I get my own share, I will go and live in town.

OJIMA. If only that foolish stranger would turn up! Why a stranger should come into this house and——

BASSI. Remember, he was your grandfather's friend.

OJIMA. At last, poor Grandfather is gone. I wonder if he knew that we only played up just to get something from his will.

AROB. Well, it didn't matter to him. He believed us, and that is why he has left his property to us. A few months ago he would rather have thrown it all into the sea.

OJIMA. Who could have thought, considering the way we treated him, that the old man had such a kindly heart! *(There is a knock. All stand.* STRANGER *enters from Grandfather's room. He is grim, dressed in black, and carries a small wooden box under his arm.)*

AROB. Stranger, how did you come out from Grandfather's room?

STRANGER. Let us not waste time on questions. This box was buried in the floor of your grandfather's room. *(He places the box on the table;* AROB *and* OJIMA *crowd together.* STRANGER *speaks sternly.)* Give me room, please. Your grandfather always wanted you to crowd around him. But no one would, until he was about to die. Step back, please. *(Both* AROB *and* OJIMA *step back.* OJIMA *accidentally steps on* AROB.*)*

AROB *(to* OJIMA*)*. Don't you step on me!

OJIMA *(querulously)*. Don't you shout at me! *(STRANGER looks at both.)*

AROB. When I sat day and night watching Grandfather in his illness, you were away in town, dancing and getting drunk. Now you want to be the first to grab at everything.

OJIMA. You liar! It was I who took care of him.

AROB. You only took care of him when you knew that he had come to some wealth.

BASSI. Why can't both of you——

AROB *(very sharply)*. Keep out of this, woman. That pretender *(pointed to* OJIMA*)* wants to bring trouble today.

OJIMA. I, a pretender? What of you, who began to scratch the old man's back simply to get his money?

AROB. How dare you insult me like that! *(He throws out a blow.*

OJIMA *parries. They fight and roll on the floor. The* STRANGER *looks on.)*

BASSI. Stranger, stop them.

STRANGER *(calmly looking at them).* Don't interfere, woman. The mills of God, the preachers tell us, grind slowly.

BASSI. I don't know anything about the mills of God. Stop them, or they will kill themselves.

STRANGER *(clapping his hands).* Are you ready to proceed with your grandfather's will, or should I wait till you are ready? *(They stop fighting and stand up, panting.)* Before I open this box, I want to know if all your grandfather's wishes have been kept. Was he buried with honour?

AROB. Yes, the greatest burial any old man has had in this village.

OJIMA. You may well answer, but I spent more money than you did.

AROB. No, you did not. I called the drummers and the dancers.

OJIMA. I arranged for the shooting of guns.

AROB. I paid for the wine for the visitors and the mourners.

OJIMA. I——

STRANGER. Please, brothers, wait. I ask you again, Was the old man respectably buried?

BASSI. I can swear to that. His grandsons have sold practically all they have in order to give him a grand burial.

STRANGER. That is good. I shall now open the box. *(There is silence. He opens the box and brings out a piece of paper.)*

AROB *(in alarm).* Where are the jewels, the money, the treasure?

STRANGER. Sh! Listen. This is the will. Perhaps it will tell us where to find everything. Listen to this.

AROB. But you cannot read. Give it to me.

OJIMA. Give it to me.

STRANGER. I can read. I am a schoolteacher.

AROB. Did you write this will for Grandfather?

STRANGER. Questions are useless at this time. I did not.

AROB. Stop talking, man. Read it.

STRANGER (reading). Now, my grandsons, now that I have been respectably and honourably buried, as all grandsons should do to their grandfathers, I can tell you a few things.

First of all, I have discovered no treasure at all. There was never anything like the "Jewels of the Shrine." (AROB *makes a sound as if something had caught him in the throat.* OJIMA *sneezes violently.*) There was no treasure hidden in the farm or anywhere else. I have had nothing in life, so I can only leave you nothing. The house which you now live in was my own. But I sold it some months ago and got a little money for what I needed. That money was my "Jewels of the Shrine." The house belongs now to the stranger who is reading this will to you. He shall take possession of this house two days after the will has been read. Hurry up, therefore, and pack out of this house. You young puppies, do you think I never knew that you had no love for me, and that you were only playing up in order to get the money which you believed I had acquired?

When I was a child, one of my first duties was to respect people who were older than myself. But you have thrown away our traditional love and respect for the elderly person. I shall make you pay for it. Shame on you, young men, who believe that because you can read and write, you need not respect old age as your forefathers did! Shame on healthy young men like you, who let the land go to waste because they will not dirty their hands with work!

OJIMA (furiously). Stop it, Stranger, stop it, or I will kill you! I am undone. I have not got a penny left. I have used all I had to feed him and to bury him. But now I have not even got a roof to stay under. You confounded Stranger, how dare you buy this house?

STRANGER. Do you insult me in my own house?

AROB (miserably). The old cheat! He cheated us to the last. To think that I scratched his back only to be treated like this!

We are now poorer than he had ever been.

OJIMA. It is a pity. It is a pity.

STRANGER. What is a pity?

OJIMA. It is a pity we cannot dig him up again. *(Suddenly a hoarse, unearthly laugh is heard from somewhere. Every-body looks in a different direction. They listen. And then again . . .)*

VOICE. Ha—ha—ha—ha! *(They all look up.)* Ha—ha—ha—ha! *(The voice is unmistakably Grandfather* OKORIE'S *voice. Seized with terror, everybody except* BASSI *runs in confusion out of the room, stumbling over the table, box, and every-thing. As they run away, the voice continues.)* Ha—ha—ha —ha! *(*BASSI, *though frightened, boldly stands her ground. She is very curious to know whether someone has been play-ing them a trick. The voice grows louder.)* Ha—ha—ha—ha! *(*BASSI, *too, is terrorized, and runs in alarm off the stage.)* Ha—ha—ha—ha!!!

(Curtain.)

FOR DISCUSSION

1. Before Okorie dies, what is his main concern?

2. Besides telling us at the beginning of the play that Okorie is "about eighty years of age," the playwright shows us that Okorie is a very old man by his actions. What evidence are we given that Okorie is advanced in years?

3. Plays about death are usually sad. Would you describe *The Jewels of the Shrine* as sad? What word or words would you use to describe it?

4. At one point in the play, Arob and Ojimway imitate Okorie (page 34). Are they making fun of him? When we imi-tate people, are we usually making fun of them, or showing that we like them? What do the words *mimic* and *emulate* mean?

5. Find an incident in the play that illustrates the saying, "There is no honor among thieves."

6. Bassi has a fairly small part in the play. In practical, every-day terms we can see a need for her because a feeble old man would probably need a housekeeper. But there is also a *dramatic* need for a character like her. In terms of communicating with the audience, what is Okorie able to do with Bassi present that he could not do without her?

7. The provisions of Okorie's will could have been either Okorie's idea or the Stranger's. Give reasons why either one would profit from designing such a will. Whose idea do you think it was? What makes you think so?

8. How would you describe the society in which this play takes place? What kinds of things happen in a society such as this that are important to the plot of the play?

9. It is said that human nature is much the same all over the world, whether in an African village, an American suburb, or a European city. How is this generalization borne out by *The Jewels of the Shrine*? What traits of human nature are shown in the play that are familiar to you? Do you see any unfamiliar traits?

10. Do you think that Okorie's revenge was justified? List some reasons which suggest that it was justified, and some which suggest that it was not. Then be prepared to take a stand on one side or the other. Your teacher will set up a panel group to discuss this matter.

FOR COMPOSITION

1. The folk language of all peoples is filled with sayings. Some of these are good luck wishes, such as the Irish saying, "May the wind be always at your back." Others resemble curses. At one point in the play, Okorie utters good luck wishes to express his satisfaction with Bassi. For example, he says, "When far-seeing owls hoot the menace of future days, let their evil prophecies keep off your path."

Try to write three good luck wishes similar to Okorie's, using a bird, an animal, or a fish in the way he used owls.

2. *A*. Suppose that Okorie and some of his old friends had gotten together and written out a "Guide for Young People Living with Old People." Working with a group of two or three classmates, write six to eight rules that might appear in such a guide.

   B. Now see if you can write three or four rules for treating old people in *your own* society.

3. Like many old people, Okorie looks back on the "good old days." Assume that you are living 50 years from now and that the "good old days" you're looking back on are the time you're living in now. Write a diary entry for 50 years from today, recalling some experiences from the present period of your life.

4. The introductory note to this play refers to "characters on both sides of the generation gap." What do you understand by the term *generation gap*? How is the "gap" shown in *The Jewels of the Shrine*? Is there a generation gap in the United States today? What makes you think so? Write a composition explaining how you think the generation gap can be eliminated, or at least narrowed and made less difficult for both sides.

A SPECIAL ACTIVITY

What do old people like to read about? Form an editorial board with a group of friends and decide what kinds of things would be interesting to old people. Then gather an assortment of articles, poems, stories, cartoons, and ads that they might like to read. Paste them on pages to make a "magazine" for old people. Each member of the editorial board should also write one article for the magazine. Think of a good title for it. One member of your group may know an old person who would like to have the magazine after you've finished making it.

THE VALIANT

HOLWORTHY HALL
and ROBERT MIDDLEMASS

THE VALIANT

If you decided to write a recipe for courage, would you include a few spoonfuls of stubbornness?

Most people probably would not, since courage is a good trait whereas stubbornness is not. As you read the first few pages of *The Valiant*, see whether you think Dyke is a courageous man or a stubborn man. When you finish reading the play, try to decide which came first, his courage or his stubbornness.

Unlike the first two plays, *The Valiant* was intended for the stage. Imagine yourself sitting in a theater, looking at a stage that has been transformed into the warden's office in a state prison. The opening comments on the weather should help to put you in the right mood for the play.

CHARACTERS

WARDEN HOLT, about sixty

FATHER DALY, the prison chaplain

JAMES DYKE, the prisoner

JOSEPHINE PARIS, the girl, about eighteen

DAN, a jailer

ATTENDANT

(Scene: The WARDEN'S *office in the State's Prison at Wethersfield, Connecticut.)*

(Time: About half-past eleven on a rainy night.)

(The Curtain rises upon the WARDEN'S *office in the State's Prison at Wethersfield, Connecticut. It is a large, cold, unfriendly apartment, with bare floors and staring, whitewashed walls; it is furnished only with the* WARDEN'S *flattopped desk and swivel-chair, with a few straight-backed chairs, one beside the desk and others against the walls, with a water-cooler, and an eight-day clock. On the* WARDEN'S *desk are a telephone, a row of electric push-buttons, and a bundle of forty or fifty letters. At the back of the room are two large windows, crossed with heavy bars; at the left there is a door to an anteroom, and at the right there are two doors. The more distant leads to the office of the deputy warden, and the nearer is seldom used.* WARDEN HOLT, *dressed in a dark brown sack suit, with a negligee shirt and a black string-tie carelessly knotted in a bow, is seated at his desk, reflectively smoking a long, thin cigar. He is verging toward sixty, and his responsibilities have printed themselves in italics upon*

his countenance. His brown hair and bushy eyebrows are heavily shot with gray; there is a deep parenthesis of wrinkles at the corners of his mouth and innumerable fine lines about his eyes. His bearing indicates that he is accustomed to rank as a despot, and yet his expression is far from that of an unreasoning tyrant. He is no sentimentalist, but he believes that in each of us there is a constant oscillation of good and evil; and that all evil should be justly punished in this world, and that all good should be generously rewarded—in the next.)

(Behind the WARDEN, *the prison* CHAPLAIN *stands at one of the barred windows, gazing steadily out into the night.* FATHER DALY *is a slender, white-haired priest of somewhat more than middle age; he is dressed in slightly shabby clericals. His face is calm, intellectual, and inspiring; but just at this moment, it gives evidence of a peculiar depression.)*

(The WARDEN *blows a cloud of smoke to the ceiling, inspects the cigar critically, drums on the desk, and finally peers over his shoulder at the* CHAPLAIN. *He clears his throat and speaks brusquely.)*

THE WARDEN. Has it started to rain?

FATHER DALY *(answers without turning).* Yes, it has.

THE WARDEN *(glaring at his cigar and impatiently tossing it aside).* It *would* rain tonight. *(His tone is vaguely resentful, as though the weather had added a needless fraction to his impatience.)*

FATHER DALY *(glances at a big silver watch).* It's past eleven o'clock. *(He draws a deep breath and comes slowly to the center of the room.)* We haven't much longer to wait.

THE WARDEN. No, thank God! *(He gets up, and goes to the water-cooler; with the glass half-way to his lips, he pauses.)* Was he quiet when you left him?

FATHER DALY *(a trifle abstractedly).* Yes, yes, he was perfectly calm and I believe he'll stay so to the very end.

THE WARDEN (*finishes his drink, comes back to his desk, and lights a fresh cigar*). You've got to hand it to him, Father; I never saw such nerve in all my life. It isn't bluff, and it isn't a trance, either, like some of 'em have—it's plain nerve. You've certainly got to hand it to him. (*He shakes his head in frank admiration.*)

FATHER DALY (*sorrowfully*). That's the pity of it—that a man with all his courage hasn't a better use for it. Even now, it's very difficult for me to reconcile his character, as I see it, with what we know he's done.

THE WARDEN (*continues to shake his head*). He's got my goat, all right.

FATHER DALY (*with a slight grimace*). Yes, and he's got mine, too.

THE WARDEN. When he sent for you tonight, I hoped he was going to talk.

FATHER DALY. He did talk, very freely.

THE WARDEN. What about?

FATHER DALY (*smiles faintly, and sits beside the desk*). Most everything.

THE WARDEN (*looks up quickly*). Himself?

FATHER DALY. No. That seems to be the only subject he isn't interested in.

THE WARDEN (*sits up to his desk, and leans upon it with both elbows*). He still won't give you any hint about who he really is?

FATHER DALY. Not the slightest. He doesn't intend to, either. He intends to die as a man of mystery to us. Sometimes I wonder if he isn't just as much of a mystery to himself.

THE WARDEN. Oh, he's trying to shield somebody, that's all. James Dyke isn't his right name—we know that; and we know all the rest of his story is a fake, too. Well, where's his motive? I'll tell you where it is. It's to keep his family and his friends, wherever they are, from knowing what's happened to him. Lots of 'em have the same idea but I never knew one to carry it as far as this before. You've certainly got to hand it to him. All we know is that we've got a man under sentence; and we don't know who he is, or where he comes from, or anything else about him, any more than we did four months ago.

FATHER DALY. It takes moral courage for a man to shut himself away from his family and his friends like that. They would have comforted him.

THE WARDEN. Not necessarily. What time is it?

FATHER DALY. Half-past eleven.

THE WARDEN (*rises and walks over to peer out of one of the barred windows*). I guess I'm getting too old for this sort of thing. A necktie party didn't use to bother me so much; but every time one comes along nowadays, I've got the blue devils beforehand and afterward. And this one is just about the limit.

FATHER DALY. It certainly isn't a pleasant duty even with the worst of them.

THE WARDEN (*wheels back abruptly*). But what gets *me* is why I should hate this one more than any of the others. The boy is guilty as hell.

FATHER DALY. Yes, he killed a man. "Willfully, feloniously, and with malice aforethought."

THE WARDEN. And he pleaded guilty. So he deserves just what he's going to get.

FATHER DALY. That is the law. But has it ever occurred to you, Warden, that every now and then when a criminal behaves in a rather gentlemanly fashion to us, we instinctively think of him as just a little less of a criminal?

THE WARDEN. Yes, it has. But all the same, this front of his makes me as nervous as the devil. He pleaded guilty all right, but he don't *act* guilty. I feel just as if tonight I was going to do something every bit as criminal as he did. I can't help it. And when I get to feeling like that, why, I guess it's pretty nearly time I sent in my resignation.

FATHER DALY *(reflectively)*. His whole attitude has been very remarkable. Why, only a few minutes ago I found myself comparing it with the fortitude that the Christian martyrs carried to their death, and yet—

THE WARDEN. He's not a martyr.

FATHER DALY. I know it. And he's anything in the world but a Christian. That was just what I was going to say.

THE WARDEN. Has he got any religious streak in him at all?

FATHER DALY. I'm afraid he hasn't. He listens to me very attentively, but— *(He shrugs his shoulder.)* It's only because I offer him companionship. Anybody else would do quite as well—and any other topic would suit him better.

THE WARDEN. Well, if he wants to face God as a heathen, *we* can't force him to change his mind.

FATHER DALY *(with gentle reproach)*. No, but we can never give up trying to save his immortal soul. And his soul tonight seems as dark and foreboding to me as a haunted house would seem to the small boys down in Wethersfield. But I haven't given up hope.

THE WARDEN. No—you wouldn't.

FATHER DALY. Are you going to talk with him again yourself?

THE WARDEN *(opens a drawer of his desk, and brings out a large envelope)*. I'll have to. I've still got some Liberty Bonds that belong to him. *(He gazes at the envelope, and smiles grimly.)* That was a funny thing—when the newspaper syndicate offered him twenty-five hundred for his autobiography, he jumped at it so quick I was sure he wanted the money for something or other. *(He slaps the envelope on the desk.)* But now the bonds are here, waiting for him, he won't say what to do with 'em. Know why? *(FATHER DALY shakes his head.)* Why, of course you do! Because the story he wrote was pure bunk from start to finish and the only reason he jumped at the chance of writing it was so's he could pull the wool over everybody's head a little farther. He don't want the bonds, but I've got to do *something* with 'em. *(He pushes a button on the desk.)* And besides, I want to make one more try at finding out who he is.

FATHER DALY. Shall I go with you to see him or do you want to see him alone?

THE WARDEN *(sits deliberating with one hand at his forehead, and the other hand tapping the desk).* Father, you gave me a thought—I believe I'm going to do something tonight that's never been done before in this prison—that is to say —not in all the twenty-eight years that *I've* been warden.

FATHER DALY. What's that?

THE WARDEN. Because maybe if he sits here awhile with just you and me, and we go at him right, he'll loosen up and tell us about himself. It'll be different from being in his cell; it'll be sort of free and easy, and maybe he'll weaken. And then, besides, if we take him to the scaffold through this passageway, maybe I can keep the others quiet. If they don't know when the job's being done, they may behave 'emselves. I don't want any such yelling and screeching tonight as we had with that Greek. *(A JAILER in blue uniform enters from the deputy's room and stands waiting.)* Dan, I want you to get Dyke and bring him to me here. *(The JAILER stares blankly at him and the WARDEN's voice takes on an added note of authority.)* Get Dyke and bring him to me.

THE JAILER. Yes, sir. *(He starts to obey the order but halts in the doorway and turns as the WARDEN speaks again. It is apparent that the WARDEN is a strict disciplinarian of the prison staff.)*

THE WARDEN. Oh, Dan!

THE JAILER. Yes, sir?

THE WARDEN. How nearly ready are they?

THE JAILER. They'll be all set in ten or fifteen minutes, sir. Twenty minutes at the outside.

THE WARDEN (*very sharp and magisterial*). Now, I don't want any hitch or delay in this thing tonight. If there is, somebody's going to get in awful Dutch with me. Pass that along.

THE JAILER. There won't be none, sir.

THE WARDEN. When everything's ready—not a second before—you let me know.

THE JAILER. Yes, sir.

THE WARDEN. I'll be right here with Dyke and Father Daly.

THE JAILER (*eyes widening*). Here?

THE WARDEN (*peremptorily*). Yes, here!

THE JAILER (*crushes down his astonishment*). Yes, sir.

THE WARDEN. When everything and everybody is ready, you come from the execution room through the passage (*He gestures toward the nearer door on the right.*)—open that door quietly—and stand there.

THE JAILER. Yes, sir.

THE WARDEN. That'll be the signal for us to start—understand?

THE JAILER. Yes, sir.

THE WARDEN (*draws a deep breath*). All right. Now bring Dyke to me.

THE JAILER. Yes, sir. (*He goes out dazedly.*)

FATHER DALY. What about the witnesses and the reporters?

THE WARDEN. They're having their sandwiches and coffee now—the deputy'll have 'em seated in another ten or fifteen minutes. Let 'em wait. (*His voice becomes savage.*) I'd like to poison the lot of 'em. Reporters! Witnesses! (*The telephone bell rings.*) Hello—yes—yes—what's that?—Yes, yes, right here—who wants him? (*To* FATHER DALY:) Father, it's the Governor! (*His expression is tense.*)

FATHER DALY (*his voice also giving evidence of incredulity and hope*). What! (*He walks swiftly over to the desk.*) Is it about Dyke?

THE WARDEN. Ssh. (*He turns to the telephone.*) Yes, this is Warden Holt speaking. Hello—oh, hello, Governor Fuller, how are you? Oh, I'm between grass and hay, thanks. Well, this isn't my idea of a picnic exactly—yes—yes— Oh, I should say in about half an hour or so—everything's just about ready. (*His expression gradually relaxes, and* FATHER DALY, *with a little sigh and shake of the head, turns away.*) Oh, no, there won't be any slip-up—yes, we made the regular tests, one this afternoon and another at nine o'clock tonight— Oh, no, Governor, nothing can go wrong— Well, according to the law I've got to get it done as soon as possible after midnight, but you're the Governor of the state— How long?—Certainly, Governor, I can hold it off as long as you want me to— What say?—A *girl!*—You're going to send her to me?—You *have* sent her!—She ought to be here by this time?—All right, Governor. I'll ring you up when it's over. Good-bye. (*He hangs up the receiver, mops his forehead with his handkerchief, and turns to* FATHER DALY *in great excitement.*) Did you get *that?* Some girl thinks Dyke's her long-lost brother, and she's persuaded the old man to let her come out here tonight—he wants me to hold up the job until she's had a chance to see him. She's due here any minute, he says—in his own car—escorted by his own private secretary! Can you beat it?

FATHER DALY (*downcast*). Poor girl!

THE WARDEN (*blots his forehead vigorously*). For a minute there I thought it was going to be a reprieve at the very last. Whew!

FATHER DALY. So did I.

(*The door from the deputy's room is opened, and* DYKE

comes in, followed immediately by the JAILER. DYKE *halts just inside the door and waits passively to be told what to do next. He has a lean, pale face, with a high forehead, good eyes, and a strong chin; his mouth is ruled in a firm straight line. His wavy hair is prematurely gray. His figure has the elasticity of youth, but he might pass among strangers either as a man of forty, or as a man of twenty-five, depending upon the mobility of his features at a given moment. He is dressed in a dark shirt open at the throat, dark trousers without belt or suspenders, and soft slippers. The* JAILER *receives a nod from the* WARDEN, *and goes out promptly, closing the door behind him.)*

THE WARDEN (*swings half-way around in his swivel-chair*). Sit down, Dyke. (*He points to the chair at the right of his desk.*)

DYKE. Thanks. (*He goes directly to the chair and sits down.*)

THE WARDEN (*leans back, and surveys him thoughtfully;* FATHER DALY *remains in the background*). Dyke, you've been here under my charge for nearly four months and I want to tell you that from the first to last you've behaved yourself like a gentleman.

DYKE (*his manner vaguely cynical without being in the least impertinent*). Why should I make you any trouble?

THE WARDEN. Well, you *haven't* made me any trouble, and I've tried to show what I think about it. I've made you every bit as comfortable as the law would let me.

DYKE. You've been very kind to me. (*He glances over his shoulder at the* CHAPLAIN.) And you, too, Father.

THE WARDEN. I've had you brought in here to stay from now on. (DYKE *looks inquiringly at him.*) No, you won't have to go back to your cell again. You're to stay right here with Father Daly and me.

DYKE (*carelessly*). All right.

THE WARDEN (*piqued by this cool reception of the distinguished favor*). You don't seem to understand that I'm doing something a long way out of the ordinary for you.

DYKE. Oh, yes, I do, but maybe *you* don't understand why it doesn't give me much of a thrill.

FATHER DALY (*comes forward*). My son, the Warden is only trying to do you one more kindness.

DYKE. I know he is, Father, but the Warden isn't taking very much of a gamble. From now on, one place is about the same as another.

THE WARDEN. What do you mean?

DYKE (*his voice very faintly sarcastic*). Why, I mean that I'm just as much a condemned prisoner here as when I was in my cell. That door (*He points to it.*) leads right *back* to my cell. Outside those windows are armed guards every few feet. You yourself can't get through the iron door in that anteroom (*He indicates the door to the left.*) until somebody on the outside unlocks it; and I know as well as you do where *that* door (*He points to the nearer door on the right.*) leads to.

THE WARDEN (*stiffly*). Would you rather wait in your cell?

DYKE. Oh, no, this is a little pleasanter. Except—

THE WARDEN. Except what?

DYKE. In my cell, I could smoke.

THE WARDEN (*shrugs his shoulders*). What do you want—cigar or cigarette?

DYKE. A cigarette, if it's all the same.

(*The* WARDEN *opens a drawer of his desk, takes out a box of cigarettes, removes one and hands it to* DYKE. *The* WARDEN, *striking a match, lights* DYKE's *cigarette, and then carefully puts out the match.*)

DYKE (*smiles faintly*). Thanks. You're a good host.

THE WARDEN. Dyke, before it's too late I wish you'd think over what Father Daly and I've said to you so many times.

DYKE. I've thought of nothing else.

THE WARDEN. Then—as man to man—and this is your last chance—who are you?

DYKE (*inspects his cigarette*). Who am I? James Dyke—a murderer.

THE WARDEN. That isn't your real name and we know it.

DYKE. You're not going to execute a name—you're going to execute a *man*. What difference does it make whether you call me Dyke or something else?

THE WARDEN. You had another name once. What was it?

DYKE. If I had, I've forgotten it.

FATHER DALY. Your mind is made up, my son?

DYKE. Yes, Father, it is.

THE WARDEN. Dyke.

DYKE. Yes, sir?

THE WARDEN. Do you see this pile of letters? (*He places his hand over it.*)

DYKE. Yes, sir.

THE WARDEN (*fingers them*). Every one of these letters is about the same thing and all put together we've got maybe four thousand of 'em. These here are just a few samples.

DYKE. What about them?

THE WARDEN. We've had letters from every State in the Union and every province in Canada. We've had fifteen or twenty from England, four or five from France, two from Australia, and one from Russia.

DYKE. Well?

THE WARDEN (*inclines toward him*). Do you know what every one of those letters says—what four thousand different people are writing to me about?

DYKE. No, sir.

THE WARDEN (*speaks slowly and impressively*). Who *are* you—and are you the missing son—or brother—or husband—or sweetheart?

DYKE (*flicks his cigarette ashes to floor*). Have you answered them?

THE WARDEN. No, I couldn't. I want you to.

DYKE. How's that?

THE WARDEN. I want you to tell me who you are. (DYKE *shakes his head.*) Can't you see you *ought* to do it?

DYKE. No, sir, I can't exactly see that. Suppose you explain it to me.

THE WARDEN (*suddenly*). You're trying to shield somebody, aren't you?

DYKE. Yes—no, I'm not!

THE WARDEN (*glances at* FATHER DALY *and nods with elation*). Who is it? Your family?

DYKE. I said I'm not.

THE WARDEN. But first, you said you were.

DYKE. That was a slip of the tongue.

THE WARDEN (*has grown persuasive*). Dyke, just listen to me a minute. Don't be narrow, look at this thing in a big, broad way. Suppose you should tell me your real name, and I publish it. It'll bring an awful lot of sorrow, let's say, to *one* family, *one* home, and that's your own. That's probably what you're thinking about. Am I right? You want to spare your family and I don't blame you. On the surface, it sure would look like a mighty fine thing for you to do. But look at it *this* way: Suppose you came out with the truth, flat-footed; why, you might put all that sorrow into *one* home —your own—but at the same time you'd be putting an immense amount of relief in four thousand others. Don't you get that? Don't you figure you owe something to all these other people?

DYKE. Not a thing.

FATHER DALY *(has been fidgeting)*. My boy, the Warden is absolutely right. You do owe something to the other people —you owe them peace of mind—and for the sake of all those thousands of poor, distressed women, who imagine God knows what, I beg of you to tell us who you are.

DYKE. Father, I simply can't do it.

FATHER DALY. Think carefully, my boy, think very carefully. We're not asking out of idle curiosity.

DYKE. I know that, but please don't let's talk about it any more. *(To the* WARDEN:*)* You can answer those letters whenever you want to, and you can say I'm not the man they're looking for. That'll be the truth, too. Because I haven't any mother—or father—or sister—or wife—or sweetheart. That's fair enough, isn't it?

FATHER DALY *(sighs wearily)*. As you will, my son.

THE WARDEN. Dyke, there's one more thing.

DYKE. Yes?

THE WARDEN. Here are the Liberty Bonds *(He takes up the large envelope from his desk.)* that belong to you. Twenty-five hundred dollars in real money.

DYKE *(removes the bonds and examines them)*. Good-looking, aren't they?

THE WARDEN *(casually)*. What do you want me to do with them?

DYKE. Well, I can't very well take them with me, so, under the circumstances, I'd like to put them where they'll do the most good.

THE WARDEN *(more casually yet)*. Who do you want me to send 'em to?

DYKE *(laughs quietly)*. Now, Warden Holt, you didn't think you were going to catch me that way, did you?

THE WARDEN *(scowls)*. Who'll I send 'em to? I can't keep 'em here, and I can't destroy 'em. What do you want to do with 'em?

DYKE (*ponders diligently and tosses the envelopes to the desk*). I don't know. I'll think of something to do with them. I'll tell you in just a minute. Is there anything else?

THE WARDEN. Not unless you want to make some sort of statement.

DYKE. No, I guess I've said everything. I killed a man and I'm not sorry for it—that is, I'm not sorry I killed that particular person. I—

FATHER DALY (*raises his hand*). Repentance—

DYKE (*raises his own hand in turn*). I've heard that repentance, Father, is the sickbed of the soul—and mine is very well and flourishing. The man deserved to be killed; he wasn't fit to live. It was my duty to kill him, and I did it. I'd never struck a man in anger in all my life, but when I knew what that fellow had done, I knew I had to kill him, and I did it deliberately and intentionally—and carefully. I knew what I was doing, and I haven't any excuse—that is, I haven't any excuse that satisfied the law. Now, I learned pretty early in life that whatever you do in this world you have to pay for in one way or another. If you kill a man, the price you have to pay is this (*He makes a gesture which sweeps the entire room.*) and that (*He points to the nearer door on the right.*) and I'm going to pay it. That's all there is to that. And an hour from now, while my body is lying in there, if a couple of angel policemen grab my soul and haul it up before God—

FATHER DALY (*profoundly shocked*). My boy, my boy, please—

DYKE. I beg your pardon, Father, I don't mean to trample on anything that's sacred to you, but what I do mean to say is this: If I've got to be judged by God Almighty for the crime of murder, I'm not afraid, because the other fellow will certainly be there, too, won't he? And when God hears the whole story and both sides of it, which *you* never heard and never will—and they never heard it in the court room, either—why, then, if he's any kind of a God at all, I'm willing to take my chances with the other fellow. That's how concerned I am about the hereafter. And, if it'll make you feel any better, Father, why I *do* rather think there's going to be a hereafter. I read a book once that said a milligram of musk will give out perfume for seven thousand years, and a milligram of radium will give out light for *seventy* thousand. Why shouldn't a soul—mine, for instance —live more than twenty-seven? But if there isn't any hereafter—if we just die and are dead and that's all—why, I'm still not sorry and I'm not afraid, because I'm quits with the other fellow—the law is quits with me, and it's all balanced on the books. And that's all there is to that. (*An* ATTENDANT *enters from the anteroom.*)

THE WARDEN. Well? What is it?

THE ATTENDANT. Visitor to see you, sir. With a note from Governor Fuller. (*He presents it.*)

THE WARDEN (*barely glances at the envelope*). Oh! A young woman?

THE ATTENDANT. Yes, sir.

THE WARDEN. Is Mrs. Case there?

THE ATTENDANT. Yes, sir.

THE WARDEN. Have the girl searched, and then take her into the anteroom and wait till I call you.

THE ATTENDANT. Yes, sir. (*He goes out.*)

THE WARDEN. Dyke, a young woman has just come to see you —do you want to see her?

DYKE. I don't think so. What does she want?

THE WARDEN. She thinks maybe she's your sister, and she's come a thousand miles to find out.

DYKE. She's wrong. I haven't any sister.

THE WARDEN (*hesitates*). Will I tell her that, or do you want to tell it to her yourself?

DYKE. Oh, you tell her.

THE WARDEN. All right. *(He starts to rise but resumes his seat as* DYKE *speaks.)*

DYKE. Just a second—she's come a thousand miles to see me, did you say?

THE WARDEN. Yes, and she's got special permission from the Governor to talk to you—that is, with my O.K.

DYKE. A year ago, nobody'd have crossed the street to look at me, and now they come a thousand miles!

FATHER DALY. This is one of your debts to humanity, my boy. It wouldn't take you two minutes to see her, and, if you don't, after she's made that long journey in hope and dread and suffering—

DYKE. Where can I talk with her—here?

THE WARDEN. Yes.

DYKE. Alone? *(The* WARDEN *is doubtful.)* Why, you don't need to be afraid. I haven't the faintest idea who the girl is, but if she happens to be some poor misguided sentimental fool, with a gun or a pocket full of cyanide of potassium, she's wasting her time. I wouldn't cheat the sovereign state of Connecticut for anything in the world—not even to please a young lady.

THE WARDEN. Dyke, there's something about you that gets everybody.

DYKE. How about the jury?

THE WARDEN. You've got a sort of way with you—

DYKE. How about that spread-eagle attorney?

THE WARDEN. I'm going to let you talk with that girl in here—alone.

DYKE. Thanks.

THE WARDEN. It's a sort of thing that's never been done before, but if I put you on your honor—

DYKE *(cynically).* My honor! Thank you, so much.

FATHER DALY. Warden, are you sure it's wise?

DYKE. Father, I'm disappointed in you. Do you imagine I'd do anything that could reflect on Warden Holt—or you—or the young lady—or *me?*

THE WARDEN. Father, will you take Dyke into the deputy's room? I want to speak to the young lady first.

FATHER DALY. Certainly. Come, my boy. (FATHER DALY *and* DYKE *start toward the deputy's room.*)

THE WARDEN. I'll call you in just a couple of minutes.

DYKE. We promise not to run away. (*They go out together.*)

THE WARDEN (*calls*). Wilson! (*The* ATTENDANT *enters from the left.*)

THE ATTENDANT. Yes, sir.

THE WARDEN. Is the girl there?

THE ATTENDANT. Yes, sir.

THE WARDEN. Frisked?

THE ATTENDANT. Yes, sir.

THE WARDEN (*throws away his cigar*). Bring her in.

THE ATTENDANT. Yes sir. (*He speaks through the door at the left.*) Step this way, Miss. This here's the Warden.

(*A young girl appears on the threshold, and casts about in mingled curiosity and apprehension. She is fresh and wholesome, and rather pretty; but her manner betrays a certain spiritual aloofness from the ultra-modern world—a certain delicate reticence of the flesh—which immediately separates her from the metropolitan class. Indeed, she is dressed far too simply for a metropolitan girl of her age; she wears a blue tailored suit with deep white cuffs and a starched white sailor-collar, and a small blue hat which fits snugly over her fluffy hair. Her costume is not quite conservative enough to be literally old-fashioned, but it hints at the taste and repression of an old-fashioned home. She is neither timid nor aggressive; she is unself-conscious. She looks at the* WARDEN *squarely, but not in boldness, and yet not in feminine appeal; she has rather the fearlessness of a girl who has lost none of her illusions about men in general. Her expression is essen-*

tially serious; it conveys, however, the idea that her serious-
ness is due to her present mission, and that ordinarily she
takes an active joy in the mere pleasure of existence.)

THE WARDEN *(had expected a very different type of visitor, so*
that he is somewhat taken aback). All right, Wilson.

THE ATTENDANT. Yes, sir. *(He goes out.)*

THE WARDEN *(with grave deference, half rises).* Will you sit
down?

THE GIRL. Why—thank you very much. *(She sits in the chair*
beside the desk and regards him trustfully.)

THE WARDEN *(is palpably affected by her youth and innocence,*
and is not quite sure how best to proceed, but eventually
makes an awkward beginning). You've had an interview
with the Governor, I understand?

THE GIRL. Yes, sir. I was with him almost an hour.

THE WARDEN. And you want to see Dyke, do you?

THE GIRL. Yes, sir. I *hope* I'm not—too late.

THE WARDEN. No, you're not too late. *(He is appraising her*
carefully.) But I want to ask you a few questions beforehand. *(Her reaction of uncertainty induces him to soften*
his tone.) There isn't anything to get upset about. I just
want to make it easier for you, not harder. Where do you
live?

THE GIRL. In Ohio.

THE WARDEN *(very kindly).* What place?

THE GIRL. In Pennington, sir. It's a little town not far from
Columbus.

THE WARDEN. And you live out there with your father and
mother?

THE GIRL. No, sir—just my mother and I. My father died when
I was a little baby.

THE WARDEN. Why didn't your mother come here herself, instead of sending you?

THE GIRL. She couldn't. She's sick.

THE WARDEN. I see. Have you any brothers or sisters?

THE GIRL *(slightly more at ease)*. Just one brother, sir—this one. He and I were the only children. We were very fond of each other.

THE WARDEN. He was considerably older than you?

THE GIRL. Oh, yes. He's ten years older.

THE WARDEN. Why did he leave home?

THE GIRL. I don't really know, sir, except he just wanted to be in the city. Pennington's pretty small.

THE WARDEN. How long is it since you've seen him?

THE GIRL. It's eight years.

THE WARDEN *(his voice almost paternal)*. As long as that? Hm! And how old are you now?

THE GIRL. I'm almost eighteen.

THE WARDEN *(repeats slowly)*. Almost eighteen. Hm! And are you sure after all this time you'd recognize your brother if you saw him?

THE GIRL. Well—*(She looks down, as if embarrassed to make the admission.)*—of course I *think* so, but maybe I couldn't. You see, I was only a little girl when he went away—he wasn't a bad boy, sir, I don't think he could ever be really bad—but if this *is* my brother, why he's been in a great deal of trouble and you know that trouble makes people look different.

THE WARDEN. Yes, it does. But what makes you think this man Dyke may be your brother—and why didn't you think of it sooner? The case has been in the papers for the last six months.

THE GIRL. Why, it wasn't until last Tuesday that Mother saw a piece in the *Journal*—that's the Columbus paper—that he'd written all about himself, and there was one little part of it that sounded so like Joe—like the funny way he used to say things—and then there was a picture that looked the least little *bit* like him—well Mother just wanted me to come East and find out for sure.

THE WARDEN. It's too bad she couldn't come herself. She'd probably know him whether he'd changed or not.

THE GIRL. Yes, sir. But I'll do the best I can.

THE WARDEN. When was the last time you heard from him, and where was he, and what was he doing?

THE GIRL. Why, it's about five or six years since we had a letter from Joe. He was in Seattle, Washington.

THE WARDEN. What doing?

THE GIRL. I don't remember. At home, though, he worked in the stationery store. He liked books.

THE WARDEN (*suspiciously*). Why do you suppose he didn't write home?

THE GIRL. I—couldn't say. He was just—thoughtless.

THE WARDEN. Wasn't in trouble of any kind?

THE GIRL. Oh, *no!* Never. That is—unless he's—here now.

THE WARDEN (*deliberates*). How are you going to tell him?

THE GIRL. I don't know what you mean.

THE WARDEN. Why, you say maybe you wouldn't know him even if you saw him—and I'll guarantee this man Dyke won't help you out very much. How do you think you're going to tell? Suppose he don't want to be recognized by you or anybody else. Suppose he's so ashamed of himself he—

THE GIRL. I'd thought of that. I'm just going to talk to him— ask him questions—about things he and I used to do to- gether—I'll watch his face, and if he's my brother, I'm sure I can tell.

THE WARDEN (*with tolerant doubt*). What did you and your brother ever used to do that would help you out now?

THE GIRL. He used to play games with me when I was a little girl, and tell me stories—that's what I'm counting on mostly —the stories.

THE WARDEN. I'm afraid—

THE GIRL. Especially Shakespeare stories.

THE WARDEN. Shakespeare!

THE GIRL. Why, yes. He used to get the plots of the plays—all the Shakespeare plays—out of a book by a man named Lamb, and then he'd tell me the stories in his own words. It was wonderful!

THE WARDEN. I'm certainly afraid he—

THE GIRL. But best of all he'd learn some of the speeches from the plays themselves. He liked to do it—he was sure he was going to be an actor or something—he was in all the high school plays, always. And then he'd teach some of the speeches to me, and we'd say them to each other. And one thing—every night he'd sit at the side of my bed, and when I got sleepy there were two speeches we'd always say to each other, like good-night—two speeches out of *Romeo and Juliet*, and then I'd go to sleep. I can see it all. (*The* WARDEN *shakes his head.*) Why do you do that?

THE WARDEN. This boy isn't your brother.

THE GIRL. Do you think he isn't?

THE WARDEN. I *know* he isn't.

THE GIRL. How do you?

THE WARDEN. This boy never heard of Shakespeare—much less learned him. (*He presses a button on his desk.*) Oh, I'll let you see him for yourself, only you might as well be prepared. (*The* ATTENDANT *enters from the anteroom.*) Tell Dyke and Father Daly to come in here—they're in the deputy's room.

THE ATTENDANT. Yes, sir. (*He crosses behind the* WARDEN, *and goes off to the right.*)

THE WARDEN. If he turns out to be your brother—which he won't—you can have, say, an hour with him. If he don't, you'll oblige me by cutting it as short as you can.

THE GIRL. You see, I've got to tell Mother something perfectly definite. She's worried so long about him, and—and *now* the suspense is perfectly terrible for her.

THE WARDEN. I can understand that. You're a plucky girl.

THE GIRL. Of course, it would be awful for us if this *is* Joe, but even that would be better for Mother than just to stay awake nights, and wonder and wonder, and never *know* what became of him. (*The* ATTENDANT *opens the door of the deputy's room, and when* DYKE *and* FATHER DALY *have come in, he crosses again behind the* WARDEN, *and is going out at the left when the* WARDEN *signs to him and he stops.*)

THE WARDEN (*gets to his feet*). Dyke, this is the young lady that's come all the way from Pennington, Ohio, to see you.

DYKE (*who has been talking in an undertone to* FATHER DALY, *raises his head quickly*). Yes, sir?

THE WARDEN. I've decided you can talk with her here—alone. (*The* GIRL *has risen, breathless, and stands fixed;* DYKE *inspects her coldly from head to foot.*)

DYKE. Thank you. It won't take long.

THE WARDEN (*has been scanning the* GIRL'S *expression; now sees that she has neither recognized* DYKE *nor failed to recognize him, and makes a little grimace in confirmation of his own judgment*). Father Daly and I'll stay in the deputy's office. We'll leave the door open. Wilson, you stand in the anteroom with the door open.

DYKE (*bitterly*). My honor!

THE WARDEN. What say?

DYKE. I didn't say anything.

THE WARDEN (*to the* GIRL). Will you please remember what I told you about the time?

THE GIRL. Oh, yes, sir.

THE WARDEN. Come, Father. (*They go off into the deputy's room, and the* ATTENDANT, *at a nod from the* WARDEN, *goes off at left.*)

(DYKE *and the* GIRL *are now facing each other;* DYKE *is well-poised and insouciant and gives the impression of complete indifference to the moment. The* GIRL, *on the other hand, is deeply agitated and her agitation is gradually increased by* DYKE's *own attitude.*)

THE GIRL (*after several efforts to speak*). Mother sent me to see you.

DYKE (*politely callous*). Yes?

THE GIRL (*compelled to drop her eyes*). You see, we haven't seen or heard of my brother Joe for ever so long, and Mother thought—after what we read in the papers—

DYKE. That I might be your brother Joe?

THE GIRL (*obviously relieved*). Yes, that's it.

DYKE. Well, you can easily see that I'm not your brother, can't you?

THE GIRL (*stares at him again*). I'm not sure. You look a little like him, just as the picture in the paper did, but then again, it's so long—(*She shakes her head dubiously.*) and I'd thought of Joe so differently—

DYKE (*his manner somewhat indulgent, as though to a child*). As a matter of fact, I couldn't be *your* brother, or anybody else's brother, because I never had a sister. So that rather settles it.

THE GIRL. Honestly?

DYKE. Honestly.

THE GIRL (*unconvinced, becomes more appealing*). What's your real name?

DYKE. Dyke—James Dyke.

THE GIRL. That's sure enough your name?

DYKE. Sure enough. You don't think I'd tell a lie at this stage of the game, do you?

THE GIRL (*musing*). No, I don't believe you would. Where do you come from—I mean where were you born?

DYKE. In Canada, but I've lived all over.

THE GIRL. Didn't you ever live in Ohio?

DYKE. No. Never.

THE GIRL. What kind of work did you do—what was your business?

DYKE. Oh, I'm sort of Jack-of-all-trades. I've been everything a man *could* be—except a success.

THE GIRL. Do you like books?

DYKE. Books?

THE GIRL. Yes—books to read.

DYKE. I don't read when there's anything better to do. I've read a lot here.

THE GIRL. Did you ever sell books—for a living, I mean?

DYKE. Oh, no.

THE GIRL (*growing confused*). I hope you don't mind my asking so many questions. But I—

DYKE. No—go ahead, if it'll relieve your mind any.

THE GIRL. You went to school somewhere, of course—high school?

DYKE. No, I never got that far.

THE GIRL. Did you ever want to be an actor? Or *were* you ever?

DYKE. No, just a convict.

THE GIRL (*helplessly*). Do you know any poetry?

DYKE. Not to speak of.

THE GIRL (*delays a moment, and then, watching him very earnestly, recites just above her breath*).

Thou knowst the mask of night is on my face
Else would a maiden blush bepaint my cheek

For that which—
(Realizing that DYKE'S *expression is one of utter vacuity she falters, and breaks off the quotation, but she continues to watch him unwaveringly.)*
Don't you know what that is?

DYKE. No, but to tell the truth, it sounds sort of silly to *me*. Doesn't it to you?

THE GIRL *(her intonation becoming slightly forlorn. But she gathers courage, and puts him to one more test.)*
Good-night, good-night, parting is such sweet sorrow
That I shall say good-night till it be morrow.

DYKE *(his mouth twitching in amusement).* Eh?

THE GIRL. What comes next?

DYKE. Good Lord, *I* don't know.

THE GIRL *(gazes intently, almost imploringly, at him as though she is making a struggle to read his mind. Then she relaxes and holds out her hand.).* Good-bye. You—you're *not* Joe, are you? I—had to come and find out, though. I hope I've not made you too unhappy.

DYKE *(ignores her hand).* You're not going now?

THE GIRL *(spiritless).* Yes. I promised the—is he the Warden, that man in there?—I said I'd go right away if you weren't my brother. And you aren't, so—

DYKE. You're going back to your mother?

THE GIRL. Yes.

DYKE. I'm surprised that she sent a girl like you on a sorry errand like this, instead of—

THE GIRL. She's very sick.

DYKE. Oh, that's too bad.

THE GIRL *(twisting her handkerchief).* No, she's not well at all. And most of it's from worrying about Joe.

DYKE. Still, when you tell her that her son isn't a murderer—at least, that he isn't *this* one—that'll comfort her a good deal, won't it?

THE GIRL (*reluctantly*). Yes, I think maybe it will, only—

DYKE. Only what?

THE GIRL. I don't think Mother'll ever be *really* well again until she finds out for certain where Joe is and what's become of him.

DYKE (*shakes his head compassionately*). Mothers ought not to be treated like that. I wish I'd treated *mine* better. By the way, you didn't tell me what your name is.

THE GIRL. Josephine Paris.

DYKE (*is suddenly attentive*). Paris? That's an unusual name. I've heard it somewhere, too.

THE GIRL. Just like the name of the city—in France.

DYKE (*knitting his brows*). And your brother's name was Joseph?

THE GIRL. Yes—they used to call us Joe and Josie—that's funny, isn't it?

DYKE (*thoughtfully*). No, I don't think it's so very funny. I rather like it. (*He passes his hand over his forehead as if trying to coerce his memory.*)

THE GIRL. What's the matter?

DYKE (*frowning*). I was thinking of something—now, what on earth was that boy's name! Wait a minute, don't tell me—wait a minute—I've got it! (*He punctuates his triumph with one fist in the palm of the other hand.*) Joseph Anthony Paris!

THE GIRL (*amazed*). Why, that's his name! That's Joe! How did you ever—

DYKE (*his manner very forcible and convincing*). Wait! Now listen carefully to what I say, and don't interrupt me, because we've only got a minute, and I want you to get this all straight, so you can tell your mother. When the war came along I enlisted and I was overseas for four years—with the Canadians. Early one morning we'd staged a big trench raid, and there was an officer who'd been wounded coming back, and was lying out there in a shell-hole under fire. The Jerries were getting ready for a raid of their own, so they were putting down a box barrage with light guns and howitzers and a few heavies. This officer was lying right in the middle of it. Well, all of a sudden a young fellow dashed out of a trench not far from where I was, and went for that officer. He had to go through a curtain of shells and more than that, they opened on him with rifles and machine guns. The chances were just about a million to one against him, and he must have known it, but he went out just the same. He got a few yards when a five-point-nine landed right on top of the two of them. Afterward, we got what was left—the identification tag was still there—and that was the name—Joseph Anthony Paris!

THE GIRL. Joe—my brother Joe—is dead?

DYKE. On the field of battle. It was one of the wonderful, heroic things that went almost unnoticed, as so many of them did. If an officer had seen it, there'd have been a decoration for your mother to keep and remember him by.

THE GIRL. And you were there—and saw it?

DYKE. I was there and saw it. It was three years ago. That's why you and your mother haven't heard from him. And if you don't believe what I've said, why, you just write up to Ottawa and get the official record. Of course, (*He shrugs his shoulders contemptuously.*) those records are in terribly poor shape, but at least they can tell you what battalion he fought with, when he went overseas. Only you mustn't be surprised no matter whether they say he was killed in action, or died of wounds, or is missing, or even went through the whole war with his outfit, and was honorably discharged. They really don't know what happened to half the men. But I've told you the truth. And it certainly ought to make your mother happy when she knows that her boy died as a soldier, and not as a criminal.

THE GIRL (*is transfigured*). Yes, yes, it will!

DYKE. And does it make you happy, too?

THE GIRL (*nods repeatedly*). Yes. So happy—after what we were both afraid of—I can't even cry—yet. (*She brushes her eyes with her handkerchief.*) I can hardly wait to take it to her.

DYKE (*struck by a sudden inspiration*). I want to give you something else to take to her. (*He picks up from the desk the envelope containing the Liberty Bonds and seals it.*) I want you to give this to your mother from me. Tell her it's from a man who was at Vimy Ridge and saw your brother die, so it's sort of a memorial for him. (*He touches her arm as she absently begins to tear open the envelope.*) No, don't you open it—let *her* do it.

THE GIRL. What is it? Can't I know?

DYKE. Never mind now, but give it to her. It's all I've got in the world and it's too late now for me to do anything else with it. And have your mother buy a little gold star to wear for her son—and you get one, too, and wear it—here—(*He touches his heart.*) Will you?

THE GIRL. Yes—I will. And yet somehow I'll almost feel that I'm wearing it for you, too.

DYKE (*shakes his head soberly*). Oh, no! You mustn't ever do that. I'm not fit to be mentioned in the same breath with a boy like your brother, and now I'm afraid it *is* time for you to go. I'm sorry, but—you'd better. I'm glad you came before it was too late, though.

THE GIRL (*gives him her hand*). Good-bye, and thank you. You've done more for me—and Mother—than I could possibly tell you. And—and I'm so sorry for you—so *truly sorry*—I wish I could only do something to make you a tiny bit happier, too. Is there anything I could do?

DYKE (*stares at her and by degrees becomes wistful*). Why—yes, there is. Only I—(*He leaves the sentence uncompleted.*)

THE GIRL. What is it?

DYKE (*looks away*). I can't tell you. I never should have let myself think of it.

THE GIRL. Please tell me. I want you to. For—for Joe's sake, tell me what I can do.

DYKE (*his voice low and desolate*). Well—in all the months I've been in this hideous place, you're the first girl I've seen. I didn't expect to see one again. I'd forgotten how much like angels women look. I've been terribly lonesome tonight, especially, and if you really do want to do something for me—for your brother's sake—you see, you're going to leave me in just a minute and—and I haven't any sister of my own, or anybody else, to say good-bye to me—so, if you could—*really* say good-bye—(*She gazes at him for a moment, understands, flushes, and then slowly moves into his outstretched arms. He holds her close to him, touches his lips to her forehead twice, and releases her.*)

DYKE (*thickly*). Good-bye, my dear.

THE GIRL. Good night. (*She endeavors to smile, but her voice catches in her throat.*) Good-bye.

DYKE (*impulsively*) What is it?

THE GIRL (*shakes her head*). N-nothing.

DYKE. Nothing?

THE GIRL (*clutches her handkerchief tight in her palm*). I was thinking—I was thinking what I used to say to my brother —for good night. (*She very nearly breaks down.*) If I *only* could have—have said it to him just once more—for good-bye.

DYKE. What was it?

THE GIRL. I—I told it to you once, and you said it was silly.

DYKE (*softly*). Say it again.

THE GIRL (*cannot quite control her voice*).

> Good-night, good-night, parting is such sweet sorrow
> That I shall say good-night till it be morrow.

(She goes uncertainly toward the anteroom, hesitates, almost turns back, and then with a choking sob she hurries through the door and closes it behind her. For several seconds DYKE *stands rigidly intent upon that door; until at length, without changing his attitude or his expression, he speaks very tenderly and reminiscently.)*

Sleep dwell upon thine eyes, peace in thy breast;
Would *I* were sleep and peace, so sweet to rest.

(The WARDEN *and* FATHER DALY *come in quietly from the deputy's room; and as they behold* DYKE, *how rapt and unconscious of them he is, they look at each other, questioningly. The* WARDEN *glances at the clock and makes as though to interrupt* DYKE's *solitary reflections but* FATHER DALY *quietly restrains him.)*

(The CHAPLAIN *sits down in one of the chairs at the back wall; the* WARDEN *crosses on tip-toe and sits at his desk; he is excessively nervous and he continually refers to the clock.* DYKE *turns, as though unwillingly, from the door; there are depths in his eyes, and his thoughts are evidently far away. He sits in the chair to the right of the* WARDEN's *desk and leans outward, his right hand on his knee. He puts his left hand to his throat as though to protect it from a sudden pain. He gazes straight ahead into the unknown and speaks in reverie.)*

Of all the wonders that I yet have heard,
It seems to me most strange that men should fear;
Seeing that death, a necessary end,
Will come when it will come.

(He stops and muses for a time, while the WARDEN *glances perplexedly at* FATHER DALY *to discover if the priest can interpret what* DYKE *is saying.* FATHER DALY *shakes his head. Abruptly* DYKE's *face is illumined by a new and welcome*

recollection; and again he speaks, while the WARDEN *tries in vain to comprehend him.*)

    Cowards die many times before their death;
    The valiant never taste of death but once.

(*He stops again and shudders a trifle; his head droops and he repeats, barely above a whisper.*)

    The valiant never taste of death but once.

(*The nearer door on the right is opened noiselessly and the* JAILER, *in obedience to his instructions, steps just inside the room and stands there mute.* FATHER DALY *and the* WARDEN *glance at the* JAILER, *and with significance at each other, and both rise, tardily. The* WARDEN's *hand, as it rests on his desk, is seen to tremble. There is a moment of dead silence; presently* DYKE *lifts his head and catches sight of the motionless* ATTENDANT *at the open door. With a quick intake of his breath, he starts half out of his seat and stares, fascinated; he sinks back slowly, and turns his head to gaze first at* FATHER DALY *and then at the* WARDEN. *The* WARDEN *averts his eyes, but* FATHER DALY's *expression is of supreme pity and encouragement. Involuntarily,* DYKE's *hand again goes creeping upward toward his throat, but he arrests it. He grasps the arms of his chair and braces himself; he rises then, and stands very erect, in almost the position of a soldier at attention.*)

THE WARDEN (*swallows hard*). Dyke!

FATHER DALY (*brushes past the* WARDEN, *his right hand lifted as though in benediction*). My son!

DYKE (*regards them fixedly, his voice low and steady*). All right, let's go.

(*He faces about, and with his head held proud and high, and his shoulders squared to the world, he moves slowly toward the open door.* FATHER DALY, *with the light of his calling in his eyes, steps in line just ahead of* DYKE. *The*

WARDEN, *his mouth set hard, falls in behind. When they have all gone forward a pace or two,* FATHER DALY *begins to speak, and* DYKE *to reply.* FATHER DALY'S *voice is strong and sweet; and* DYKE *speaks just after him, not mechanically, but in brave and unfaltering response.)*

FATHER DALY. "I will lift up mine eyes unto the hills . . . "

DYKE. "The valiant never taste of death but once."

FATHER DALY. "From whence cometh my help."

DYKE. "The valiant never taste of death but once."

FATHER DALY (*has almost reached the door; his voice rising a semi-tone, and gaining in emotion*). "My help cometh from the Lord which made Heaven and earth."

DYKE. "The valiant never taste of death—but once."

(*When the* WARDEN, *whose hands are tightly clenched, has passed the threshold, the* JAILER *follows and closes the door behind him. There is a very brief pause and then . . .*)

(*Curtain.*)

FOR DISCUSSION

1. The title, *The Valiant*, comes from two famous lines in William Shakespeare's *Julius Caesar*:
   Cowards d· many times before their death;
   The valiant never taste of death but once.
   What do these lines mean?
2. We learn many things about Dyke before he appears on stage. What are two things we find out about his character or personality before we see him?
3. Why does Dyke refuse to reveal his true identity? Do you agree with his reasons?
4. How did Dyke protect his story about Joseph Paris so that

if the girl and her mother checked it they would not know it was a false story?

5. Although Dyke is a convicted murderer, the audience is supposed to feel sorry for him and like him somewhat. In what ways are we made to feel sorry for Dyke?

6. Why do you think the authors decided to have the visit to the prison made by Joe's sister instead of by his mother?

7. How many reasons can you think of for having both the Warden and the Chaplain in this play? What does each contribute to the drama?

8. The point at which the audience is certain of the outcome of a play is called the *climax*. Where does the climax occur in *The Valiant?*

9. By willfully committing murder, Dyke deliberately ignored the law. Do we ever have the right to disobey a law? Are there different kinds of laws?

10. Some states have dropped the death penalty as a punishment for certain criminal acts. Why do you suppose they have done so? Would you use *The Valiant* as an argument for or against capital punishment? Explain.

FOR COMPOSITION

1. Suppose that Dyke left a note in his cell before his sister came to visit him. The note told the Warden what to do with the Liberty Bonds. What would it say? Write the note that Dyke might have left.

2. The girl tells the Warden that the uncertainty has made her mother sick. The mother would rather hear some bad news than remain unsure of her son's whereabouts. Would you rather hear bad news than be uncertain about something? Write a short paper giving reasons why you would prefer bad news—or uncertainty. Try to recall a personal experience which you can use to support your position.

3. In your judgment, is the main purpose of prison to punish prisoners, to rehabilitate them, or a combination of the two? Write a one-paragraph paper indicating what you think the chief purpose of prison is.

Scene V from

ABE LINCOLN IN ILLINOIS

ROBERT E. SHERWOOD

ABE LINCOLN IN ILLINOIS

"And how far do you think you will go with anyone like Abe Lincoln, who is lazy and shiftless and prefers to stop constantly along the way to tell jokes?"

This is the question Elizabeth Edwards asks her sister, Mary Todd, when Mary reveals that she intends to marry Abraham Lincoln. As you read the selection that follows, notice Mary's reasons for deciding that Lincoln should be her husband. Do you consider these good reasons for getting married?

This selection is an excerpt from a three-act, biographical play, *Abe Lincoln In Illinois*, by Robert E. Sherwood. In the play, which covers Lincoln's life from his youth until he is inaugurated as President in 1861, Sherwood tries to give a realistic rather than a heroic picture of Lincoln. After reading this scene, you may wish to read the whole play. It was awarded the Pulitzer Prize for drama in 1939.

CHARACTERS

NINIAN EDWARDS

ELIZABETH EDWARDS, wife of Ninian

MARY TODD, sister of Elizabeth

MAID

ABE LINCOLN

(*Place: The parlor of the Edwards house in Springfield.*)

(*Time: An evening in November, some six months after the preceding scene.*)

(*Scene: There is a fireplace at the right, a heavily curtained bay window at the left, a door at the back leading into the front hall. At the right, by the fireplace, are a small couch and an easy chair. There is another couch at the left, and a table and chairs at the back. There are family portraits on the walls. It is all moderately elegant.*)

(NINIAN *is standing before the fireplace, in conversation with* ELIZABETH, *his wife. She is high-bred, ladylike—excessively so. She is, at the moment, in a state of some agitation.*)

ELIZABETH. I cannot believe it! It is an outrageous reflection on my sister's good sense.

NINIAN. I'm not so sure of that. Mary has known Abe for several months, and she has had plenty of chance to observe him closely.

ELIZABETH. She has been entertained by him, as we all have. But she has been far more attentive to Edwin Webb and Stephen Douglas and many others who are distinctly eligible.

NINIAN. Isn't it remotely possible that she sees more in Abe than you do?

ELIZABETH. Nonsense! Mr. Lincoln's chief virtue is that he hides no part of his simple soul from any one. He's a most amiable creature, to be sure; but as the husband of a high-bred, high spirited young lady . . .

NINIAN. Quite so, Elizabeth. Mary is high-spirited! That is just why she set her cap for him. (ELIZABETH *looks at him sharply, then laughs.*)

ELIZABETH. You're making fun of me, Ninian. You're deliberately provoking me into becoming excited about nothing.

NINIAN. No, Elizabeth—I am merely trying to prepare you for a rude shock. You think Abe Lincoln would be overjoyed to capture an elegant, cultivated girl, daughter of the President of the Bank of Kentucky, descendant of a long line of English gentlemen. Well, you are mistaken . . .

(MARY TODD *comes in. She is twenty-two—short, pretty, remarkably sharp. She stops short in the doorway, and her suspecting eyes dart from* ELIZABETH *to* NINIAN.)

MARY. What were you two talking about?

NINIAN. I was telling your sister about the new song the boys are singing:

"What is the great commotion, motion,

Our country through?

It is the ball a-rolling on

For Tippecanoe and Tyler, too—for Tippecanoe . . ."

MARY (*with a rather grim smile*). I compliment you for thinking quickly, Ninian. But you were talking about me! (*She looks at* ELIZABETH, *who quails a little before her sister's determination.*) Weren't you?

ELIZABETH. Yes, Mary, we were.

MARY. And quite seriously, I gather.

NINIAN. I'm afraid that our dear Elizabeth has become unduly alarmed . . . .

ELIZABETH. Let me say what I have to say! (*She turns to* MARY.) Mary—you must tell me the truth. Are you—have you ever given one moment's serious thought to the possibility of marriage with Abraham Lincoln? (MARY *looks at each of them, her eyes flashing.*) I promise you, Mary, that to me such a notion is too far beyond the bounds of credibility to be . . .

MARY. But Ninian has raised the horrid subject, hasn't he? He has brought the evil scandal out into the open, and we must face it, fearlessly. Let us do so at once, by all means. I shall answer you, Elizabeth: I have given more than one moment's thought to the possibility you mentioned—and I have decided that I shall be Mrs. Lincoln. (*She seats herself on the couch.* NINIAN *is about to say, "I told you so," but thinks better of it.* ELIZABETH *can only gasp and gape.*) I have examined, carefully, the qualifications of all the young gentlemen, and some of the old ones, in this neighborhood. Those of Mr. Lincoln seem to me superior to all others, and he is my choice.

ELIZABETH. Do you expect me to congratulate you upon this amazing selection?

MARY. No! I ask for no congratulations, nor condolences, either.

ELIZABETH (*turning away*). Then I shall offer none.

NINIAN. Forgive me for prying, Mary—but have you as yet communicated your decision to the gentleman himself?

MARY (*with a slight smile at* NINIAN). Not yet. But he is coming to call this evening, and he will ask humbly for my hand in marriage; and, after I have displayed the proper amount of surprise and confusion, I shall murmur, timidly, "Yes!"

ELIZABETH. You make a brave jest of it, Mary. But as for me, I am deeply and painfully shocked. I don't know what to say to you. But I urge you, I beg you, as your elder sister, responsible to our father and our dead mother for your welfare . . .

MARY (*with a certain tenderness*). I can assure you, Elizabeth—it is useless to beg or command. I have made up my mind.

NINIAN. I admire your courage, Mary, but I should like . . .

ELIZABETH. I think, Ninian, that this is a matter for discussion solely between my sister and myself!

MARY. No! I want to hear what Ninian has to say. (*To* NINIAN.) What is it?

NINIAN. I only wondered if I might ask you another question.

MARY (*calmly*). You may.

NINIAN. Understand, my dear—I'm not quarreling with you. My affection for Abe is eternal—but I'm curious to know—what is it about him that makes you choose him for a husband?

MARY (*betraying her first sign of uncertainty*). I should like to give you a plain, simple answer, Ninian. But I cannot.

ELIZABETH (*jumping at this*). Of course you cannot! You're rushing blindly into this. You have no conception of what it will mean to your future.

MARY. You're wrong about that, Elizabeth. This is not the result of wild, tempestuous infatuation. I have not been swept off my feet. Mr. Lincoln is a Westerner, but that is his only point of resemblance to Young Lochinvar. I simply feel that of all the men I've ever known, he is the one whose life and destiny I want most to share.

ELIZABETH. Haven't you sense enough to know you could never be happy with him? His breeding—his background—his manner—his whole point of view . . . ?

MARY (*gravely*). I could not be content with a "happy marriage" in the accepted sense of the word. I have no craving for comfort and security.

ELIZABETH. And have you a craving for the kind of life you

would lead? A miserable cabin, without a servant, without a stitch of clothing that is fit for exhibition in decent society?

MARY (*raising her voice*). I have not yet tried poverty, so I cannot say how I should take to it. But I might well prefer it to anything I have previously known—so long as there is forever before me the chance for high adventure—so long as I can know that I am always going forward, with my husband, along a road that leads across the horizon. (*This last is said with a sort of mad intensity.*)

ELIZABETH. And how far do you think you will go with any one like Abe Lincoln, who is lazy and shiftless and prefers to stop constantly along the way to tell jokes?

MARY (*rising; furious*). He will not stop, if I'm strong enough to make him go on! And I am strong! I know what you expect of me. You want me to do precisely as you have done —and marry a man like Ninian—and I know many, that are just like him! But with all due respect to my dear brother-in-law—I don't want that—and I won't have it! Never! You live in a house with a fence around it—presumably to prevent the common herd from gaining access to your sacred precincts—but really to prevent you, yourselves, from escaping from your own narrow lives. In Abraham Lincoln I see a man who has split rails for other men's fences, but who will never build one around himself.

ELIZABETH. What are you saying, Mary? You are talking with a degree of irresponsibility that is not far from sheer madness . . . .

MARY (*scornfully*). I imagine it does seem like insanity to you! You married a man who was settled and established in the world, with a comfortable inheritance, and no problems to face. And you've never made a move to change your condition, or improve it. You consider it couldn't be improved. To you, all this represents perfection. But it doesn't to me!

I want the chance to shape a new life, for myself, and for my husband. Is that irresponsibility?

(A maid appears.)

MAID. Mr. Lincoln, ma'am.

ELIZABETH. He's here.

MARY *(firmly)*. I shall see him!

MAID. Will you step in, Mr. Lincoln? *(ABE comes in, wearing a new suit, his hair nearly neat.)*

ABE. Good evening, Mrs. Edwards. Good evening, Miss Todd. Ninian, good evening.

ELIZABETH. Good evening.

MARY. Good evening, Mr. Lincoln. *(She sits on the couch at the left.)*

NINIAN. Glad to see you, Abe.

(ABE sees that there is electricity in the atmosphere of this parlor. He tries to be affably casual.)

ABE. I'm afraid I'm a little late in arriving, but I ran into an old friend of mine, wife of Jack Armstrong, the champion rowdy of New Salem. I believe you have some recollection of him, Ninian.

NINIAN *(smiling)*. I most certainly have. What's he been up to now?

ABE *(stands in front of the fireplace)*. Oh, he's all right, but Hannah, his wife, is in fearful trouble because her son Duff is up for murder and she wants me to defend him. I went over to the jail to interview the boy and he looks pretty tolerably guilty to me. But I used to give him lessons in the game of marbles while his mother foxed my pants for me. *(He turns to ELIZABETH.)* That means, she sewed buckskin around the legs of my pants so I wouldn't tear 'em to shreds going through underbrush when I was surveying. Well—in view of old times, I felt I had to take the case and do what I can to obstruct the orderly processes of justice.

NINIAN (*laughs, with some relief*). And the boy will be acquitted. I tell you, Abe—this country would be law-abiding and peaceful if it weren't for you lawyers. But—if you will excuse Elizabeth and me, we must hear the children's prayers and see them safely abed.

ABE. Why—I'd be glad to hear their prayers, too.

NINIAN. Oh, no! You'd only keep them up till all hours with your stories. Come along, Elizabeth. (ELIZABETH *doesn't want to go, but doesn't know what to do to prevent it.*)

ABE (*to* ELIZABETH). Kiss them good night, for me.

NINIAN. We'd better not tell them you're in the house, or they'll be furious.

ELIZABETH (*making one last attempt*). Mary! Won't you come with us and say good night to the children?

NINIAN. No, my dear. Leave Mary here—to keep Abe entertained. (*He guides* ELIZABETH *out, following her.*)

MARY (*with a little laugh*). I don't blame Ninian for keeping you away from those children. They all adore you.

ABE. Well—I always seem to get along well with children. Probably it's because they never want to take me seriously.

MARY. You understand them—that's the important thing. . . . But—do sit down, Mr. Lincoln. (*She indicates that he is to sit next to her.*)

ABE. Thank you—I will. (*He starts to cross to the couch to sit beside* MARY. *She looks at him with melting eyes. The lights fade.*)

. (*Curtain.*)

FOR DISCUSSION

1. Although Mary and Elizabeth are sisters, they are very different in their attitudes, outlooks, and values. What are their differences? Just why does Mary wish to become Abraham Lincoln's wife? What are Elizabeth's objections to him?

2. What does Ninian think about Elizabeth's attitude toward Mary?

3. What does Mary mean when she says that she will display "the proper amount of surprise and confusion" before accepting Lincoln's proposal of marriage? Does this statement tell us anything about Mary?

4. We see Abraham Lincoln very briefly in this selection, but we see him long enough to glimpse some of his good qualities. Name two of these. Does he seem to have any weak qualities?

5. Lincoln says that he will defend Duff Armstrong in court even though he considers Duff guilty of murder. If you were a lawyer, would you defend someone whom you considered guilty? Why? Would you defend Dyke, in *The Valiant*, even though he pleaded guilty?

6. None of the four major characters in this scene is on the stage during the entire scene. Mary comes in after the scene has started; so does Abe Lincoln. Ninian and Elizabeth Edwards leave before the scene ends. What does the playwright accomplish by moving the actors on and off stage in this way?

7. This scene is from a three-act play entitled *Abe Lincoln in Illinois*. Why do you suppose that playwright Robert Sher-

wood called it that instead of *Abraham Lincoln in Illinois?*
What would be an appropriate title for this scene?

8. Suppose that it is a few years earlier and Mary is still in her
   teens. At different times, two boys call on Mrs. Edwards to
   ask permission to take Mary to a square dance. The first
   boy says, "Hi, Mrs. E., How's chances of takin' that gor-
   geous, swingin' sister of yours to the dance Saturday?" The
   second boy says, "Good evening, Mrs. Edwards. I'd like to
   ask your permission to escort Mary to the dance Saturday
   evening." Which boy is more likely to receive Mrs. Edwards'
   permission? Can we say that he is a better boy than the
   other one?

FOR COMPOSITION

1. The beginning of this scene suggests that something happens before the scene opens; the ending suggests that something comes after the scene itself. Choose one of the two
   situations described below and write some lines for it.

   a. The opening sentence, "I cannot believe it!" makes
      us think that Elizabeth and Ninian were talking
      before the curtain went up. Write 6 to 8 lines of
      dialogue to show what they might have said dur-
      ing this time. Let your last line be Elizabeth's
      statement, "I cannot believe it! It is an outrageous
      reflection on my sister's good sense."

   b. Start with Abraham Lincoln's closing line in this
      scene, "Thank you—I will," and write 8 to 10
      lines of dialogue between Mary and Abe. (Re-
      member how Mary said she was going to behave.)

2. A person who hopes to become President of the United
   States must have certain personal qualities to succeed in this
   demanding job. Write a paragraph in which you describe the
   three most important qualities that you think a future President should have.

3. Because weddings are often very formal occasions, wedding invitations are usually written in formal language. Using a composition book as a reference, write a formal invitation to the wedding of Mary Todd and Abe Lincoln.

THE WORLD ON A HILL

ALICE CHILDRESS

THE WORLD ON A HILL

What determines your behavior in a particular situation? Years of training at home? Electrical or chemical reactions in the brain over which you have no control? Getting up on the wrong side of bed? Invigorating weather? Behavioral scientists and biochemists often cannot pin down with certainty the reason for certain actions.

Playwrights, on the other hand, in order to capture your interest, must suggest why characters act the way they do. You must be given a glimpse beneath the surface to show what makes the characters do as they do.

In "The World on a Hill," Alice Childress introduces you to a spoiled brat, an ineffective mother, and a young thief. By the end of the play, you should have a pretty good notion of the reasons for their behavior.

CHARACTERS

THE WOMAN, a delicate, attractive, but unhappy white woman of thirty-five.

LIONEL, her son, who is seven and spoiled.

THE BOY, a West Indian Negro, desperate, unhappy, and sixteen.

(Place: A West Indian vacation island.)

(Time: Ten o'clock in the morning.)

(Scene: A park-like area. There is a bench at stage center, upstage right is a wall; one can look over this stone wall and down the hill to the area below. The woman shouts down to her son.)

THE WOMAN. Lionel! Lionel, get down, do you hear me? Oh, dear God! Get down from that tree!

LIONEL. No. No! Noooooo!

THE WOMAN. Do you want to break your leg again? *(Aside.)* Oh, dammit. Lionel, dear heart, listen to mother.

LIONEL. It's cooler up here!

THE WOMAN *(As she spreads a blanket and rests her picnic basket).* It is not.

LIONEL. It is!

THE WOMAN I don't have to put up with this. You get down or I'll. . .

LIONEL. Or you'll what? *(Faint sound of a police whistle blowing in the distance.)*

THE WOMAN. Get down! *(Screaming.)*

LIONEL. I hear a police whistle.

THE WOMAN. Get down before I shake you down.

LIONEL. I'm going to tell my father on you.

THE WOMAN *(After a split second of silence)*. Tell him. What do I care? What can he do to me? *(She is worried about him telling his father.)* Oh, for God's sake, when will you learn to obey? There that's a good boy. Good boys get good things because good boys speak gently to their mothers. *(She opens the picnic basket and places two paper plates on a table cloth.)* We're going to have picnic lunch. . . . *(LIONEL enters.)* Won't that be nice?

LIONEL. No. I want to go to the bottom of the hill and play with the native children down there.

THE WOMAN. You'll get in a fight.

LIONEL. I won't.

THE WOMAN. You always do.

LIONEL. No, not always.

THE WOMAN. After lunch.

LIONEL. I'm not hungry.

THE WOMAN. Oh, you're a one.

LIONEL. A one what?

THE WOMAN. But a picnic is fun.

LIONEL. It's not a real picnic with only two people.

THE WOMAN. Right here and all over the world, . . . there are so many poor little boys who would love to have this lunch.

LIONEL. Well, give it to them, I don't care. I want to go down to the bottom of the hill, I want to go down to the bottom of the hill, I want to go down to the. . . .

THE WOMAN *(Through clenched teeth)*. Oh, stop it.

LIONEL. Why'd we have to come way up here?

THE WOMAN. Lionel, I wanted to be alone with you, to talk to you. . . .

LIONEL. You said you were going to shake me out of the tree. If it's a picnic, why didn't father come? Why did you run out of the house and leave him? You'd better not shake me out of any trees.

THE WOMAN. You mustn't worry your father. Don't tell him what I said, you hear?

LIONEL *(Realizes he can strike a bargain)*. I wanta go down the hill, I wanta go. . . .

THE WOMAN. Yes, yes, go on.

LIONEL. Can I buy some candy? A man has a cart with red and green coconut bars.

THE WOMAN. He's dirty and his cart is dirty.

LIONEL. I don't care.

THE WOMAN. I have vanilla fudge in the basket and lemon cookies. . . .

LIONEL. I want a green. . . . All right. *(His pause is a threat. She gives him a coin from her purse.)*
I heard a police whistle from over that way.

THE WOMAN. Yes. Go buy your green candy. That's how people get polio.

LIONEL. But I've had injections. Save me a sandwich. Do you have baloney?

THE WOMAN. No. There's peanut butter, watercress with cheese. . . .

LIONEL. Ahhhhhhhhhhhhh. . . .*(He exits.)*

THE WOMAN. Hair of the dog. *(She takes a small flask from the bottom of the basket, mixes it with a bit of soda from a thermos and sips the drink.)* Tell his father. (THE BOY *runs up to the park bench. He is tired and out of breath, sits down on the far end of the bench. The sound of the police whistle grows fainter as it fades in the distance. The woman is startled, she reaches in the basket and holds the thermos as a weapon. The boy notices her purse on the bench beside him. The woman rises and hopes to leave.)*

THE BOY. Don't move. *(She sits down and continues to sip the drink.)* And don't scream.

THE WOMAN. I won't. You may have my purse, take it and go. Take the money and leave, I won't scream.

THE BOY. I don't want it.

THE WOMAN. Please, please don't, I beg you. . . .

THE BOY. Don't what?

THE WOMAN *(Significant silence)*.

THE BOY. I know what you mean. You must think you're some pretty. You're no movie star. I tell you. . . .

THE WOMAN. Thank God. I want to go home, if you don't mind.

THE BOY. I have a knife in my pocket, if you move, I'll cut you with it.

THE WOMAN. I won't move. You don't want my purse and you're not going to assault me, so why are you here? What do you want?

THE BOY. The park is free, I can sit here as well as you. I don't yet know what I want, but I do know I don't want you to call the police for me.

THE WOMAN. One scream, one loud scream and you'll be caught.

THE BOY. And you'll be dead. Why don't you try it?

THE WOMAN. Young man, I'm not afraid of you or . . . or death. I'm going to get up, pack my basket and walk away. You may cut me or do what you will but I'm going. . . . Being pushed around, . . . I'm sick of it, tired of it. . . . *(She starts to pack the basket. He stands over her with one hand in his pocket.)* Don't dare me or I *will* scream and it'll be the worse for you if I do, . . . and well do you know it.

THE BOY *(Takes his hand out of his pocket and turns out the lining)*. I don't have a knife. *(Turns out the other pocket.)* Nothing at all. And the only thing in this pocket is a hole. *(She sighs with relief.)* Now, why don't you yell for the police? Be white and scream.

THE WOMAN. I don't want to, believe me, I don't. Go on about your business, it's none of my concern what you've done or why they're looking for you.

THE BOY. Scream, go on and scream.

THE WOMAN. Well, I . . . I told you I don't want to.

THE BOY. Because you're afraid, afraid you'll be mixed in the affair. Perhaps you would have to go to court, . . . maybe I belong to a famous gang and they might "bump you off," . . . that's why you won't scream.

THE WOMAN. You belong to a famous gang? It's plain to see you don't belong to a famous anything.

THE BOY. You don't look so dressed up to me.

THE WOMAN. But I didn't say I belong to a famous gang. Shame on you for telling such tall tales.

THE BOY. I should have stole your purse and maybe assaulted you too, after all, if they're after me for one thing they may as well gun me down for two or three, . . . what's the difference?

THE WOMAN. Why are they after you?

THE BOY *(A strange, faraway look comes over his face).* I tried to rob the bank.

THE WOMAN. The bank? How?

THE BOY. I had cased the place, see? I walked in with my gun covered, a handkerchief over my face. . . .

THE WOMAN. Where is the gun now?

THE BOY. Ah . . . er . . . ah . . . I threw it away.

THE WOMAN. Where?

THE BOY. In the river.

THE WOMAN. What river?

THE BOY. What difference does it make?

THE WOMAN. But there's no river near here. You're lying again, aren't you?

THE BOY. Yes.

THE WOMAN. Well, I never. Can't you tell the truth at all?

THE BOY. No.

THE WOMAN. Well, honestly, I do declare, ... Why can't you?

THE BOY. It's very hard for me to tell the truth.

THE WOMAN. It must be a curse or something.

THE BOY. I'm ashamed of the truth. The truth is too terrible. . . .

THE WOMAN. Why are they looking for you? What crime did you commit? Tell me.

THE BOY. I tried to steal an orange.

THE WOMAN. Tried?

THE BOY. I dropped it while I was running.

THE WOMAN. Well. Why did you steal it?

THE BOY. I don't know.

THE WOMAN. Are you hungry?

THE BOY. No, I'm full. I had a beef dinner only a little while ago.

THE WOMAN. Where did you have your beef dinner?

THE BOY. Jeez, lady, why don't you leave me alone! Take your be-damn basket and go screaming for the police! Tell them the thief is cornered. No, I didn't have a beef dinner! Holy Saints, lady!

THE WOMAN. Are you hungry?

THE BOY. And don't go gettin' big-eyed 'bout whether I'm hungry or not. Actin' like you're the Red Cross maybe.

THE WOMAN. That's no way to live, stealing oranges, I mean, *trying* to steal oranges.

THE BOY. *Orange*, one, an orange, one damn small orange.

THE WOMAN. Running until your lungs would burst. Where is your family? Don't you have people?

THE BOY *(That look is on his face again)*. No, I have no one. My mother and father are dead, they were swept away in a hurricane. My older brother went off to sea and left me alone. His ship went down in a storm, he stayed on deck with the captain while the others took to life boats. . . .

THE WOMAN. You have people.

THE BOY. What?

THE WOMAN. You have people. Don't tell me another lie.

THE BOY. I have people.

THE WOMAN. Where are they?

THE BOY. They're all at home, mother, father and eight brothers and sisters. You're an American aren't you?

THE WOMAN. Yes. Tell me, why do you tell so many lies? Your tongue should be washed with brown soap.

THE BOY. Lady, I lie because I am black and you are white.

THE WOMAN. Oh, I see, I understand.

THE BOY. Ha, and that's the first lie you've believed, only because you're such a liar yourself. You lie too and also that George Washington. If a man is caught standing by a fallen cherry tree with an axe in his hand there's no virtue in confessing. Tell me you never lied.

THE WOMAN. Sometimes I have, everyone does at times, . . . but not like you. If there's one thing I can't abide it's a chronic liar.

THE BOY. Are you happy?

THE WOMAN. That's none of your business.

THE BOY. Because I am black. . . .

THE WOMAN. Stop saying that.

THE BOY. Black business is your business but white business is none of mine.

THE WOMAN. Talking all that nonsense. I'm happy, reasonably so.

THE BOY. You don't look happy to me. I heard you screaming at your little boy when I was hiding in the bushes. Ten miles away they must have heard you. *(Mimics her.)* "Get down! Get down! Tell your father, I don't care, get down!"

THE WOMAN. Hmmmm, sassy thing. Yelling at a child is no sign of happiness or unhappiness.

THE BOY. Are you happy?

THE WOMAN. Hmmmm, why can't we tell the truth?

THE BOY. My mother always says . . . "Know the truth and the truth will set you free." But she doesn't seem very free to me.

THE WOMAN. Why must we lie?

THE BOY. Because . . . the truth is almost impossible. The truth shames me, the truth makes other people laugh at me. The truth is hurtful.

THE WOMAN. Most likely that's so. It should be very easy for us to be truthful with one another. I don't know your name, you don't know mine and we shall probably never see each other again. Oh, there are so many things I need to say, that I've never been able to say. We could tell the truth to each other.

THE BOY. Native boy makes lady laugh. I'm not here for your amusement.

THE WOMAN. I won't laugh, I promise. Tell me some of your thoughts, what's important to you, . . . some deep truth.

THE BOY. You will laugh.

THE WOMAN. Try me. Tell me some innermost thought.

THE BOY (*His eyes glitter with pleasure*). Well, I would like to kill all the white people in the world.

THE WOMAN. Oh, no! Well, I don't know why you'd think I'd laugh at that.

THE BOY. The truth is the truth. I would like to kill them but I can't and I'll probably never kill even one.

THE WOMAN. Why?

THE BOY. Because they have everything and I have nothing.

THE WOMAN. You mustn't think such things.

THE BOY. But I do. Since I can't kill them and don't like to kill except in my mind, . . . then I wish a big war would happen and kill them for me.

THE WOMAN. The war would kill you too and so where's the profit?

THE BOY. I wouldn't care because *everybody* would be dead and that's a satisfaction.

THE WOMAN. If you were dead how would you feel satisfaction?

THE BOY. If there's a Heaven, I will be there laughing. The white people will be in Hell moaning and gnashing their teeth, consumed by fire.

THE WOMAN. Truth is quite a game.

THE BOY. Don't worry. A man threw our belongings out in the street when we couldn't pay our rent. I prayed that he would die, I prayed for a long time, . . . but he is still living and over seventy-five years old. A big war would settle matters quickly and all at once. Atomic war. . . . Whooosh! All settled, everybody the same, all equal.

THE WOMAN. War is evil. Praying for death is evil. I am for peace, my husband is for peace. He writes articles about the peoples of the world, articles that will bring about greater understanding. . . .

THE BOY. I've never read them. *(Laughs.)* Neither did our old landlord.

THE WOMAN. I don't think you've got good sense. (THE BOY *laughs.)* Would you want to kill me?

THE BOY. No.

THE WOMAN. All white people aren't bad, in fact most of them . . .

THE BOY. I don't feel like picking through them for the good ones, it's a slow job. A war would take care of matters without placing the burden on my shoulders. I'll tell you another truth about myself if you promise not to laugh.

THE WOMAN. I'm sure I won't.

THE BOY. I always imagine that I'm famous, very often I imagine until my father knocks me on the head. . . . "Stop looking like a damn idiot! What the hell you starin' at? Get up and bring some fire-wood, . . . such a be-damn good for nothing." And then my brothers and sisters laugh and mock how my mouth hangs open. *(Slants his head to one side and gapes in imitation of their mimicking)* Go on laugh if you want to.

THE WOMAN. What do you see when you imagine you're famous?

THE BOY. Different things, it's seldom the same. Sometimes I'm a doctor who has made a great discovery. I've discovered a sure cure for cancer, . . . but I'm black, see?

THE WOMAN. Yes?

THE BOY. All the white people are begging me to turn the secret over to them, . . . but I won't. . . .

THE WOMAN. No, you wouldn't.

THE BOY. . . . unless they change their ways. Then they do change and they're grateful to me because of my discovery; white people give me medals and black people send me millions of letters thanking me for what I've done to make them all free. I am chief advisor to presidents and kings, I'll visit Buckingham Palace, the Russians will give me a welcome like they do the astronauts. . . .

THE WOMAN. Until your war comes along.

THE BOY. Oh, but there'd be no need of a war. Maybe I wouldn't turn over my secret until all the countries agreed to have no wars. Sometimes I see myself as a famous movie actor, like Sydney Po-ten-nay. . . . I stand on a platform and everyone is cheering and applauding. Other times I'm just rich, for no particular reason except I was maybe born rich. I have the best of everything. I'm dressed in a fine suit, not store-bought but made for me especially.

THE WOMAN. Yes, a nice tailor-made blue suit.

THE BOY. But not navy blue.

THE WOMAN. Lighter? A soft, dusty blue.

THE BOY. I have a light tan shirt that I wear with it.

THE WOMAN. And you're going for a sail on your yacht.

THE BOY. You're laughing at me.

THE WOMAN. I'm trying to tell you that I understand.

THE BOY. Well, I wouldn't go yachting but I'd travel around in a big, private plane . . . all over the world. I'd see all there is to see and learn what there is to know; . . . I've never been out of this gritty town in my life.

THE WOMAN. I know. In my mind's eye I see myself as other than I am.

THE BOY. You see yourself in a big house with large, beautiful rooms and floors that shine.

THE WOMAN. Well, I live in a large house.

THE BOY. With shiny floors?

THE WOMAN. Yes.

THE BOY. And a flower garden, ... big shade trees?

THE WOMAN. Yes.

THE BOY. Do you ever go in those hotsy-totsy places for the tourists ... places with a canopy over the door ... soft lantern light inside ... and a band playing music?

THE WOMAN. Yes, yes, yes, but life should mean more than that.

THE BOY. Jeez, lady, what do you want? To go in a place like that and not sweat about what it's going to cost! Lady, you got nothing to dream about! You got too much for real.

THE WOMAN. I guess your dreams are more interesting. What else do you see?

THE BOY. I see myself married to a wonderful, beautiful girl and she ... well, she's crazy about me, mad about me.

THE WOMAN (*Bitterly*). And when she wants to talk to you, you won't say, "I'm busy"?

THE BOY. Oh, no.

THE WOMAN. And you'll never forget her birthday.

THE BOY. I won't.

THE WOMAN. And you won't make her life silent and empty.

THE BOY. No. It'll be a picnic.

THE WOMAN. And every day will be wonderful because you're together.

THE BOY. Oh ... I ... I guess so.

THE WOMAN. You'll never be too busy with other things to ... to. ...

THE BOY. To what?

THE WOMAN. What I said before ... to give her some of your time!

THE BOY. No.

THE WOMAN. And if there are children ... don't ... don't lead them away ... I mean don't talk to her in a manner that causes the child to . . . the children to talk to her in the same way . . . don't. . . . *(She is crying.)*

THE BOY. Don't cry, it's only make-believe.

THE WOMAN. I know.

THE BOY. I don't have a handkerchief.

THE WOMAN. I have one. *(Takes a handkerchief from her purse and dabs her eyes.)* When you speak to her your voice should be gentle . . . gentle . . . that's the meaning of *gentle*man.

THE BOY. I'm glad I told you. It's the first time I've told anybody. If things could be like I imagine, . . . a man's a man.

THE WOMAN. And a woman should be a woman, . . . damn and double damn.

THE BOY. Dreaming is silly.

THE WOMAN. It is not.

THE BOY. It is whenever you look at it like this and talk about it straight out. It loses something because, well, I don't know, even if I couldn't have a great large house, I sure would like to have a room to myself instead of sharing one with three brothers; a nicely painted, clean room. I'd also like a pair of corduroy trousers and a Sunday suit.

THE WOMAN. I'd like to have some respect shown me in my own home.

THE BOY. Gratitude, I'm sick of it. My mother says my trouble is I'm ungrateful. I am. If we mostly have beans for dinner she says I should be grateful because beans are better than nothing. She's always grateful for the rags we wear, the junk we eat.

THE WOMAN. My husband says I should be grateful that we have plenty of . . . almost everything. He can't understand why a woman who does nothing should ever be tired. Being useless and not needed . . . you get tired.

THE BOY. Can you imagine my mother so grateful for beans?

THE WOMAN. Such a silly thought.

THE BOY. Please don't talk about my mother!

THE WOMAN. I wasn't. I meant that you have a silly thought.

Maybe she just talks about being grateful because she must keep telling the lie in order to just make it from one day to the other

THE BOY Couldn't she be truthful . . . to me?

THE WOMAN. But you, of all people, know it's not easy. You could talk to her, tell her. . . .

THE BOY. No, I've never talked to them like this. They'd think I was crazy. But no matter what they thought I couldn't bring myself to do it.

THE WOMAN. They've thought many things they couldn't bring themselves to say.

THE BOY They're not at all like me. Pa just works and never says much. He's a porter in the movie house. Ma cooks and cleans and washes. They go to bed, wake up and start all over again. Every day is the same.

THE WOMAN. We're all alike, . . . afraid of the truth. Some of our dreams . . yachts and flying around the world . . . they're lies too.

THE BOY. That's not so. Some people do those things.

THE WOMAN. But it's easier to dream of a yacht than to get down to the business of obtaining a pair of corduroy trousers . . . or a moment of tenderness. There's a challenge . . . love and corduroy trousers.

THE BOY. Why don't you talk to your husband?

THE WOMAN. That's not so simple. We rarely speak to each other. No one is angry but there's nothing to say. He has his books and the boy and friends who talk about India, The United States, Israel, the Soviet Union, Korea, North and South Vietnam, . . little countries and big events.

THE BOY. That sounds great. Don't you join with them? Oh, well, I guess a woman wouldn't.

THE WOMAN. Yes, I do. His friends think I'm very intelligent, . . . but my husband knows I'm not. Every time he opens his mouth it's. . . . "Why don't you". . . . Why don't you this or that. Why don't you say this or do that.

THE BOY. Tell him.

THE WOMAN. He'd merely nod and stare off into space.

THE BOY. I wonder what he thinks.

THE WOMAN. What do you really want to do? What one thing do you want to do more than any other?

THE BOY. I want to go to school but they won't let me because I'm dumb. I am dumb.

THE WOMAN. Don't say that.

THE BOY. It's true. I'm stupid when you compare my marks with my brother's. But I'd like to go to school anyway.

THE WOMAN. Yes, you go to school and study hard.

THE BOY. There's only enough money for one to go; so the bright one goes, not me.

THE WOMAN. That's not fair. Oh, I know what it is to be surrounded by bright ones. They're out to save mankind but they don't realize that I'm mankind also.

THE BOY. We have to help my brother because he's smart, smart enough to maybe become a doctor.

THE WOMAN. Even so, we're entitled to something.

THE BOY. And I hate chopping wood and cleaning yards. That's what I do, clean up the yards to help him through school when it's me that's wanting to go. All right, I'm selfish but that's how I feel!

THE WOMAN. And I want to speak up in my house, without mincing words, without feeling like an idiot. I don't want to be in fear of him, in fear of saying the wrong thing, in fear of the boy. . . . I have rights too . . . haven't I?

THE BOY. And when I get home I'm going to tell them. . . . "Look here, don't you think, don't you dare think. . . ." (*Loses some of his resolve.*) Oh, they'll be so angry with me.

THE WOMAN. Let them. Can they bite you?

THE BOY. No, but. . . .

THE WOMAN. Can they sentence you to be hanged?

THE BOY. No, but when my father is done through hollering at me, I'd rather be bitten and hung at the same time.

THE WOMAN. Let them be angry. After all, you're angry with yourself and I'm so mad at me I could scream. Let them be as angry as they damn well please. Understand? People need to hear from us. If they're asleep we'll wake them up. We've got our rights! Ride on, young man, ride through the storm.

THE BOY (*Applauding*). Bravo! Bravo! Hear! Hear!

THE WOMAN. We're not afraid of anything! We'll tell the world!

THE BOY. Lady, I'm not a thief.

THE WOMAN. And I'm not a coward!

THE BOY. About the stealing, I woke up this morning and I knew something had to happen, I had to make a change, not tomorrow or the next but today!

THE WOMAN. Carry on! Carry on!

THE BOY. I didn't go to clean the woman's yard. I deliberately didn't.

THE WOMAN. Good for you. Didn't I walk out on Albert in the middle of one of his "Why don't you" speeches. Out, out in God's fresh air. I know what you're saying.

THE BOY. I walked around awhile, then it looked like nothing was going to happen. . . .

THE WOMAN. I know, the same old sameness.

THE BOY. . . . and I couldn't think of anything important, so I went for that orange, and I wanted them to see me doing it, because I didn't care if I was arrested and thrown into jail, . . . just so long as things would be different this evening. I couldn't stand to have another day like the others behind me. It had to be different and it is!

THE WOMAN. Damn shame. Aren't you hungry?

THE BOY. Lord, I'm starving. (*She unpacks the basket. He helps her.*) Olives! I had some olives once when my sister worked a banquet at the hotel.

THE WOMAN. Take the bottle home with you. Put it in this bag so no one will accuse you of pinching them.

THE BOY. Cake, a whole, little cake with icing. This is like Christmas, I mean a good Christmas, a prosperous Christmas.

THE WOMAN. It's a birthday cake. Today is my birthday. I'm thirty-five. You won't tell.

THE BOY. Wow! Well, that's not so old. Our landlord is sixty-five. I know another man who is eighty.

THE WOMAN. Yes, they're a little older.

THE BOY. I was sixteen a month ago. This is how I'm going to tell them. . . . *(with swagger)* "Yes, yes, I'm going to school. You can holler all you want to. . . . Well, he'll have to clean up some yards and pay for his own schooling. Oh, don't make me laugh, go on and holler but I'm telling you the truth. . . ." *(LIONEL enters, his mouth and chin covered with evidence of the green coconut bar.)*

THE WOMAN. Lionel, this is . . . is . . . is . . . er. . . .

THE BOY. Winston.

THE WOMAN. Winston, this is my son, Lionel. I'm Norma Smith.

LIONEL *(Is blaming WINSTON)*. I'm ready to go home. A boy wanted to fight me, a native boy.

THE WOMAN *(Insisting)*. Lionel, this is Winston.

LIONEL. How do you do.

THE BOY *(Answering LIONEL's attitude)*. How do you do. *I'm* a native.

LIONEL. Yes.

THE WOMAN. And so is Lionel.

THE BOY. I'll be going now.

THE WOMAN. Not until we've had lunch. Lionel, give me the rest of the green coconut.

LIONEL. No.

THE WOMAN. I'm waiting.

LIONEL. No.

THE BOY. Boy, don't you hear your mother talking to you? *(LIONEL turns over the rest of the coconut bar.)*

LIONEL (*To* WINSTON). My father knows everything about the world and all the people in it.

THE BOY. Is that so?

THE WOMAN. Not quite.

LIONEL. I don't want lunch, let's go.

THE WOMAN. I want lunch, so sit down and make yourself comfortable.

LIONEL (*Sits down*). I'm going to tell my father when I get home.

THE WOMAN. Tell him what?

LIONEL. That . . . that we had a picnic with . . . with. . . .

THE WOMAN. With Winston.

LIONEL. With Winston. I'd rather go home.

THE WOMAN. Father always says the world is getting smaller.

LIONEL. Yes, shrinking away bit by bit.

THE WOMAN. Right now it's no bigger than this hill-top.

LIONEL. Down at the bottom of the hill they caught a boy for stealing.

THE BOY. Stealing what?

LIONEL. A bottle of milk from a store.

THE BOY. Oh. (THE WOMAN *pours milk for* LIONEL *and* WINSTON).

LIONEL. What's in that other bottle? (*Meaning the liquor.*)

THE WOMAN. Stale punch, . . . but we don't want it, don't need it.

THE BOY. Why don't you light your mother's birthday candles? (THE WOMAN *lights a match, passes it to* LIONEL. *He lights the candles.*) Just like Christmas.

LIONEL. Six candles. Are you six?

THE WOMAN. No, I'm twenty-one, I'm a woman today.

LIONEL. Oh, you were always a woman. (*She starts to blow them out.*) You make wishes first!

THE WOMAN. I wish that everyone will soon have enough food to eat, enough clothing to wear. . . .

LIONEL. You're supposed to think the wish and not say it aloud.

THE WOMAN (*Looks at* THE BOY, *then closes her eyes*). A very special wish. *(Opens her eyes.)* It will come true. (LIONEL *is about to bite into a sandwich.)*

THE BOY. Don't you bless the food?

THE WOMAN. Not very often.

THE BOY. We always bless the beans. *(A jet plane passes overhead.)*

LIONEL. Look, it's a bomber!

THE WOMAN. It isn't.

LIONEL. It's carrying bombs!

THE WOMAN. No. *(She notices a trace of the old glitter in* WINSTON's *eyes.)* It's carrying medicine and other things to do us good. Winston, would you like to bless the food?

THE BOY. It's a pleasure when food's as good as this. Thank the Lord for this blessed food which we are about to receive from his bounty through his grace amen.

THE WOMAN. Well, let's go at it.

LIONEL. Mother, Winston can put a whole half of a watercress and butter in his mouth all at one shove.

THE WOMAN. Oh, Lionel. . . .

LIONEL. And so can I! *(Demonstrates.)*
                    (Curtain.)

FOR DISCUSSION

1. The contrast between a wealthy thirty-five-year-old white woman and a poor sixteen-year-old Negro boy is obvious. However, these two people are able to communicate with each other because they have much in common. What do they have in common? Give your reasons that indicate which of the two can expect a happier future.

2. Lionel gets permission to go down the hill as part of an implicit agreement that includes his not telling his father what his mother has said. Is this a bargain or blackmail? How do you distinguish between the two? Why should a mother have to bargain with or blackmail her son?

3. Most of the play is a dialogue between Mrs. Smith and Winston. What function does Lionel serve at the beginning of the play?

4. Although Mrs. Smith seems to be in danger when Winston says that he will cut her with a knife, she does not scream for the police. What reasons can you suggest for her behavior?

5. Early in his conversation with Mrs. Smith, Winston alternates between lies and the truth. Why does he? How are you able to tell when he is lying? What causes him to change?

6. At one point, Winston says, "Lady, I lie because I am black and you are white." Mrs. Smith responds, "Oh, I see. I understand." Then Winston says, "Ha, and that's the first lie you've believed. . . ." Explain what these lines mean.

7. There is little physical action indicated in *The World on a Hill*. Could a director expect to hold the audience's attention if Winston and Mrs. Smith simply sat on the bench throughout the play merely talking with each other? If not, who might move from the bench? What line or lines would be good ones to move on?

8. What does Winston mean when he says, "If a man is caught standing by a fallen cherry tree with an axe in his hand, there's no virtue in confessing"? Discuss whether you think he is right or wrong.

9. What are some reasons why Winston probably chose to cure cancer in one of his fantasies?

10. An author uses irony when he wants a situation to appear to be the opposite of what is normally expected. Just before they begin to eat, the author gives us an example of irony by comparing the habits of Mrs. Smith and Winston. What is the irony?

FOR COMPOSITION

1. It is ten years later. One of the three characters sees one of the others on a television news program and decides to write him a letter telling of his experiences during the past decade. Early in the letter, the writer should recall the meeting on the hill that took place ten years ago. Keep in mind the ages of the characters and their outlooks toward life.

2. Like *Sorry, Wrong Number*, this play causes the reader to be highly critical of a husband who does not appear on stage. "We are going to give you an opportunity to tell your side of the story, Mr. Smith." Write a composition from Mr. Smith's point of view telling what a grand person he is. Your teacher will have some of the papers read in front of the room so that the class can determine whether Mr. Smith proves that he is a fine person or not.

   "But as you prepare your defense, Mr. Smith, remember these two points. Nobody likes a person who brags too much, and husbands who are publicly critical of their wives don't score many points either."

3. Read a play, a story, a book, or a poem by a Negro writer, then write a paper indicating whom the author is speaking for. Is he speaking primarily as a member of the Negro race? As a member of the human race? As a man? As a woman? As a Negro man or woman? You may need to quote from the selection you have chosen to support your opinion.

THE JEST OF HAHALABA

OF

HAHALABA

LORD DUNSANY

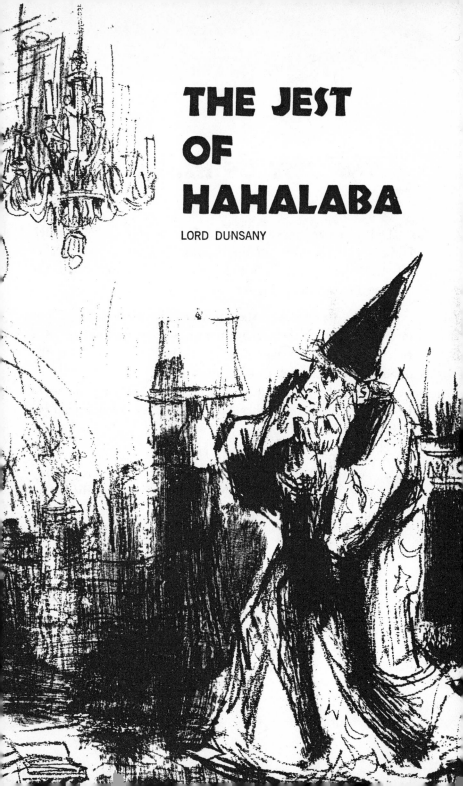

THE JEST OF HAHALABA

Did you ever make a wish and then have it come true? Perhaps you blew out *all* the candles on your birthday cake. Or maybe you broke off the big half of the wishbone. Or happened to see a shooting star.

Usually we associate such wishmaking with children, but in *The Jest of Hahalaba* the person who makes a wish is a rich old man. As a matter of fact, he pays money for the opportunity to make a wish. If you are familiar with the behavior of the genies and jinn who fulfill wishes, you should be able to predict whether Sir Arthur Strangways' paid-for wish will make him happy.

The setting for *The Jest of Hahalaba* is London in 1928. However, the play could take place almost anywhere, in any year, as long as it begins on New Year's Eve, shortly before midnight.

CHARACTERS

SIR ARTHUR STRANGWAYS

SNAGGS, his butler

AN ALCHEMIST, a kind of magician supposed to be able to change
cheap metals into gold

HAHALABA, the Spirit of Laughter

(Scene: The smoking room, SIR ARTHUR STRANGWAYS' *house in London.)*

(Time: The last moments of 1928. Bells are ringing in the New Year. SIR ARTHUR *is in an armchair. Enter* SNAGGS, *his butler.)*

SIR ARTHUR. A happy New Year to you, Snaggs.

SNAGGS. A happy New Year to you, Sir Arthur, and many of them

SIR ARTHUR. Ah, thank you, Snaggs.

SNAGGS. There's a man to see you, Sir Arthur, who . . .

SIR ARTHUR. Oh yes, yes.

SNAGGS. . . . who says he wants to see you, Sir Arthur.

SIR ARTHUR. Yes, show him up, please.

SNAGGS. He's, if I may say so, Sir Arthur, a very strange person.

SIR ARTHUR. Yes, I know. Show him up.

SNAGGS. Very strange indeed.

SIR ARTHUR. Yes, I was expecting him.

SNAGGS And it's very late, Sir Arthur.

SIR ARTHUR. Yes, never mind.

SNAGGS. As you wish, Sir Arthur.

SIR ARTHUR. Yes, show him up, please.

SNAGGS. As you wish. (*Exit, leaving* SIR ARTHUR *sitting thoughtful. Re-enter with the* ALCHEMIST *in a dull maroon cloak, elderly, bearded, and dressed like nobody later than Teniers.*)

SNAGGS. The man to see you, Sir Arthur. (SNAGGS *lingers.*)

SIR ARTHUR. Thank you, Snaggs. Thank you.

SNAGGS (*reluctantly dismissed*). Thank you, Sir Arthur.

SIR ARTHUR. You have the stuff? (ALCHEMIST *shows an old snuff-box and taps it, nodding his head.*) And the words?

ALCHEMIST (*in a sort of whisper*). Yes. (SIR ARTHUR *takes the snuff-box.*)

SIR ARTHUR (*extending hand*). Give me the words.

ALCHEMIST. They may not be written. (*Re-enter* SNAGGS.)

SNAGGS. I will wait up, Sir Arthur, in case you should ring. If you should ring I would come at once.

SIR ARTHUR. Thank you, Snaggs. Thank you. (*Exit* SNAGGS. SIR ARTHUR *goes to door and locks it.*) You will tell me the words?

ALCHEMIST. There's laws in England against the likes of me.

SIR ARTHUR. Laws?

ALCHEMIST. Any time since the days of Edward the Confessor.

SIR ARTHUR. But you will tell me the words.

ALCHEMIST. Aye. But we must proceed softly.

SIR ARTHUR. All is quiet. We may start now.

ALCHEMIST. You have another door.

SIR ARTHUR. Oh, no one ever comes that way.

ALCHEMIST. It is better locked.

SIR ARTHUR. Perhaps it is. (*He locks it.*) Now.

ALCHEMIST. The powder then is placed upon the floor in a ring, wide enough to contain two feet, and two and a half times as wide should you dare to call up Eblis.

SIR ARTHUR. No, no. I shall not call up Eblis.

ALCHEMIST. That is something, Master. That is something. That is one thing to be thankful for in all this bad business. I couldn't have borne it, Master. His mouth alone: I couldn't have borne to look at it.

SIR ARTHUR. No, no. I do not wish to see Eblis.

ALCHEMIST. I couldn't have borne to see him.

SIR ARTHUR. You shan't see him. Tell me the words.

ALCHEMIST. Well, Master, you put the powder in a ring, wide enough to hold common feet, scarce larger than ours. And then, Master, if you must, you light it. If you must, Master, if you must. And it smolders and the smoke goes away to the left and the right, and goes round the ring. And just as the two smokes meet, just then you say . . . (*He whispers.*) And you name the spirit that you would call up. And he must come. And he must grant one wish, the first demand that you make of him. And I wish I had never told you, and I wish I had never come.

SIR ARTHUR. Never mind that now. Let's get on with the business.

ALCHEMIST. Well, Master; then, there be many spirits. There's the spirit of Death, the spirit of Drought, the spirit of Fever.

SIR ARTHUR (*now preparing the ring*). No, no. I'll have some jolly spirit.

ALCHEMIST. Oh, Master, call up the spirit of Death, the spirit of Fever, even the spirit of Terror, but not the spirit of Laughter.

SIR ARTHUR. The spirit of Laughter? Why not? I like the sound of him. We'll have the spirit of Laughter.

ALCHEMIST. Oh, Master, not that spirit.

SIR ARTHUR. Why not?

ALCHEMIST. Why, Master, because all these spirits, they are all at enmity with man, and are overfull of ingenuity: it always was so. And they sit for ages planning how to prevail against man. For ages, Master. You would hardly believe it. And when they have formed a plan they won't rest until they have tried it; you would not credit their malice. And most of all are they like this, most of all when they have been compelled to grant a wish. They are like it then most of all.

SIR ARTHUR. Then we won't have the spirit of Death.

ALCHEMIST. Oh, Master, the spirit of Laughter is the worst of all but one. His contrivances are beyond the wit of all the lesser spirits. You are not making the circle too wide, Master?

SIR ARTHUR. No, no. We'll only have the spirit of Laughter.

ALCHEMIST. Be warned, Master, and have none of him.

SIR ARTHUR. Come, tell me his name.

ALCHEMIST. Be warned, Master.

SIR ARTHUR. I've paid you well for this.

ALCHEMIST. Yes, Master, but be warned.

SIR ARTHUR. His name, then.

ALCHEMIST. His name—oh, Master, call never upon this spirit— his name is Hahalaba.

SIR ARTHUR. So that's his name. The spell again. (SIR ARTHUR *now holds a matchbox.* ALCHEMIST *whispers in his ear.* SIR ARTHUR *ignites the powder and mutters the spell, ending with the name* HAHALABA. HAHALABA *steps through a curtain and stands in the ring, an athletic spirit, with a small cloak slung over his breast.*)

HAHALABA. What is your will of me?

ALCHEMIST. Oh, Master, nothing that he can turn to his advantage.

SIR ARTHUR. It shall be nothing. I have thought of all.

ALCHEMIST. Only a trifle, Master. Something too small for his contrivances, or . . .

SIR ARTHUR. It is only a trifle.

HAHALABA. What is your will of me?

SIR ARTHUR. Only a trifle. I wish to see a file of the *Times*.

HAHALABA. For what year?

SIR ARTHUR. For the year 1929.

ALCHEMIST. 1929!

HAHALABA (*pulling cloth from table and revealing a file of one year of the* Times). It is there.

SIR ARTHUR. Ha!

HAHALABA. Within an hour of midnight it will vanish.

SIR ARTHUR. Oh. We have not long then.

HAHALABA. It has far to go, and must be there by dawn.

SIR ARTHUR. Where?

HAHALABA. In the deeps of time. (*Exit.*)

SIR ARTHUR. Where has he gone?

ALCHEMIST. He has gone back.

SIR ARTHUR. To work, then.

ALCHEMIST (*as* SIR ARTHUR *gets half sheets and pencil and turns to the heap*). Oh, Master, I'm glad you asked for a little thing. It's a mercy, Master, a mercy.

SIR ARTHUR. A *little* thing, indeed!

ALCHEMIST. Aye, Master. For had you asked a great thing of such as him, he would have triumphed surely.

SIR ARTHUR. A little thing!

ALCHEMIST. Aye, Master, I know the ways of them.

SIR ARTHUR. A little thing, be damned. I shall make millions on this. Millions.

ALCHEMIST. Oh, Master, beware Hahalaba. Beware the spirit of Laughter.

SIR ARTHUR. I tell you I shall make millions. This alone, for instance, this alone: December 31st, 1929: I see he's got December on the top the way the newspaper people keep it, they put the fresh paper on top of the one of the day before all the year round, and keep the lot like *this*: this number alone is worth all the money I've got, or you either. Patangas 104. You go down to the City and buy Patangas. But you don't understand.

ALCHEMIST. Master, I go to no city guided by Hahalaba.

SIR ARTHUR. He's got nothing to do with it. He's gone. But I read in the *Times* that Patangas are 104. *(Jots down a word on half sheet, saying aloud, "Patangas.")* I shall soon know if this file is genuine by waiting a few days and checking these. *(He lays his hand on the edges at bottom of heap.)*

ALCHEMIST. Oh, it is genuine. He may not lie. But he is frivolous and cunning. I know Hahalaba.

SIR ARTHUR. If this is genuine, (Reads a line or two.) as it evidently is, I shall make millions. There we are again. Pocahontas 37. Who'd have thought it? I haven't paid you enough, old fellow. I haven't paid you enough.

ALCHEMIST. Master, I ask no more. I ask no more that comes from Hahalaba.

SIR ARTHUR. Nonsense. It comes out of the *Times*. And I'm the only man that's got a copy. November 20th this is, 1929. And the only one in the world. If you'd care for half a million you can have it. It will be nothing to me.

ALCHEMIST. No, Master. No.

SIR ARTHUR. Or a million for that matter.

ALCHEMIST. No, Master, I have no uses for it.

SIR ARTHUR. As you like. *(Lower down the file.)* And here again. Tangerines at 80. Hullo. Here's old Perrot dead. He should have kept himself fit: he was no older than me. If he'd have played golf. . . . Well, well. October 27th.— Fancy that. *(Takes another paper.)* Hullo, hullo. *(Makes brief note.)* I'll play hell with the Stock Exchange.

ALCHEMIST. Master.

SIR ARTHUR. Ha, ha! Lord! Bolivian United. Well, I never. *(Makes note.)*

ALCHEMIST. Master.

SIR ARTHUR. *And* Ecuador Guaranteed. Millions!

ALCHEMIST. Master.

SIR ARTHUR. Well.

ALCHEMIST. I have given you your desire, and you have paid me well. Our account is settled. May I go hence?

SIR ARTHUR. Go hence? Yes, if you like.

ALCHEMIST. Thank you, Master; for of all spirits of evil, I fear most the spirit of Laughter.

SIR ARTHUR. Yes, you told me that. No one's keeping you. But wait a moment. Wait a moment. There's one thing I'll give you that you'll understand how to use. Wait a moment.

ALCHEMIST. Master, I go not to that city.

SIR ARTHUR. No, it's not the City. Wait a moment. Ah, here we have it. The Derby. Aurelian won. You back Aurelian for the Derby. (*Writes on a half sheet and gives it to* ALCHEMIST.) There. Aurelian for the Derby.

ALCHEMIST. Master, I make no wager, lest in my hour of gain Hahalaba mock me. (*He puts paper down on a table.*) And Master—

SIR ARTHUR. Well, never mind now. There's only a few more minutes, and I can't waste them talking. They're worth a million a minute.

ALCHEMIST. As you will, Master.

SIR ARTHUR. Well, goodbye then, and thank you very much. (ALCHEMIST *tries the door; it is locked.*) Ah, the door. Give me a moment and I'll let you out. (*He takes key from pocket, but continues reading papers and making notes.*) Another of them. Tromkins now. Why can't they keep themselves fit? Mexican Airways Limited! Well, well. (*Another note. Hastily turns over papers, making brief notes, till he nears the bottom of the heap.*) Yes, yes. Well, that'll be enough. There's millions in it. I'll let you out now. (*Walks to the door with key in one hand, the last paper in the other.*)

ALCHEMIST. Thank you, Master, thank you.

SIR ARTHUR. And your friend Hahalaba will find it hard to laugh over this deal, for I'm the richest man in England now.

ALCHEMIST. Not yet, Master.

SIR ARTHUR. Well I soon will be. *(Unlocks door.)*

ALCHEMIST. And Master. Read no more of these hidden things. It is surely enough. Tempt Hahalaba no further.

SIR ARTHUR. I won't. I've read all I want. I've enough knowledge to put against the brains of all the financiers in London.

ALCHEMIST. Then read no further, Master. Put it down.

SIR ARTHUR. That? Do you know what that is? That is today's paper. January 1st, 1929, the last of the heap. I shall read today's paper before I go to bed. We're in 1929 now. Well, goodbye, and a happy New Year.

ALCHEMIST. Farewell, Master. *(Exit.* SIR ARTHUR *returns to his chair and settles down to the British habit of reading the day's* Times.*)*

SIR ARTHUR. Nothing of interest. Dull, I suppose, after the other. Hullo! What's this? What? What? But it can't be! But this is today's paper! But I'm alive! Good God.

(With breath coming short he goes to decanter of brandy, pours out, mixes, and drinks. He stands a little steadier, hand to heart now and then.) Bit of a shock that. Read that kind of thing. Silly Jugginses. Who can have been fool enough to invent a yarn like that? It's today's paper and I'm quite well. *(But the improvement was only momentary and he rings for* SNAGGS, *then he goes panting to the sofa and lies down.)* Bit of a . . . shock, that. *(Enter* SNAGGS. *Goes to* SIR ARTHUR *on sofa. All the copies of the* Times *have vanished.)*

SNAGGS. Hullo. What's this has happened? *(Goes to table and sees* SIR ARTHUR's *notes on half sheets.)* Patangas? Mexican Airways? Nothing to account for it there. *(Almost absently he crumples them and throws them in the fire; then turns to the business in hand.)* Now what should I do? *(A glance towards the sofa. Then he goes to the telephone.)* Ah, would you please give me the *Times*. I don't know the number. Yes, the *Times* Office, please. Is that the *Times*? Oh, could I speak to the Editor? . . . Oh, well, perhaps he'd do. But it's important. . . . Tell him something sudden. . . . Oh, yes. I'm butler to Sir Arthur Strangways. Mr. Snaggs is *my* name. . . . Well I thought you'd like to know Sir Arthur has just died. . . . Sudden like. . . . Yes. *(Leaving the phone, he passes the other table on which* ALCHEMIST *had put down his slip. He picks it up and reads.)* Aurelian for the Derby. He's no good.

(Curtain.)

FOR DISCUSSION

1. How does Snaggs try to influence Sir Arthur at the beginning of the play? What feeling did you get from Snaggs' behavior? Why is this scene important to the final outcome?

2. Why does the Alchemist take the secret formula to Sir Arthur? Why does Sir Arthur want the formula? What is the Alchemist's reason for not taking Sir Arthur's tip on the Derby?

3. What is Snaggs' attitude toward Sir Arthur at the end of the play? Is Snaggs' behavior at the end of the play consistent with his behavior at the beginning?

4. The playwright does not tell us exactly why Sir Arthur wants to have so much money. In certain ways, however, he does guide our thinking. How does he make us assume that Sir Arthur lacks good intentions?

5. None of the characters in *The Jest of Hahalaba* is a "good" person. You probably would not want to have any of them as a next-door neighbor. But can reading a play be an enjoyable experience even though all of the characters are selfish and greedy?

6. Eblis is one of the names given to the devil. Suppose that Sir Arthur had summoned Eblis. What might have happened?

7. Hahalaba is the spirit of laughter. Are there any laughs in what he does in this play? If you were to change his title from spirit of laughter to spirit of something else, what title would you give him?

8. What was the playwright's purpose in choosing New Year's Eve as the time for the play?

9. It would not be difficult to read a moral or lesson into this play. In eight words or less, make up a moral that could come from *The Jest of Hahalaba*. You may put the moral in your own words or use one that has become a common expression.

FOR COMPOSITION

1. *The Jest of Hahalaba* follows a pattern that is common in literature. It can be outlined something like this:

    a. Main characters are identified.

    b. A mysterious friend or acquaintance arrives.

    c. The acquaintance possesses a charm or talisman that enables the owner to wish for whatever he wants.

    d. One of the main characters secures the charm.

    e. The acquaintance warns this character against the evil power of the charm.

    f. The character makes a wish.

    From that point on, the plot may turn in one of two directions. If the person is greedy or silly, his wish (or wishes) will probably backfire. If he is noble and wishes for something worthy, the outcome is likely to be happy.

    Try to write a short, short story that follows the above outline. You may use either kind of ending, but drop hints along the way to suggest that the character should be either rewarded or punished. Then be sure to use an appropriate ending.

2. Snaggs is now looking for a new job and he sees the following ad in a newspaper:

    HELP WANTED—BUTLER. Good pay and pleasant working conditions. Generous vacations. Meals, clothing, and living quarters provided. Write to B. T. Smith, Box 612, The London *Times*.

    Assume that you are Snaggs. Write an answer to this ad, applying for the position. Be sure to list a few references and give your previous working experience. Also, remember that your future employer may judge you on the basis of the neatness of your letter.

3. Do you think that the Alchemist was partly responsible for what happened to Sir Arthur? Decide whether in your judgment he was (1) very much responsible, (2) partly responsible, or (3) not responsible at all. Write a paragraph giving reasons for your decision.

THE LEADER OF THE PEOPLE

JOHN STEINBECK

dramatized by

LUELLA E. McMAHON

THE LEADER OF THE PEOPLE

Time can be cruel to yesterday's heroes. The man who sets a record by hitting 61 home runs in one season is just another ballplayer the following year. A soldier who wins the Congressional Medal of Honor has trouble finding a job in civilian life.

In *The Leader of the People,* Grandfather is one of yesterday's heroes. He led a group of wagons westward when Indians and starvation threatened the wagon trains. Now he is an old man living with his memories.

When Grandfather comes to the home of his married daughter for a two-week stay, his visit causes a conflict within the family. As you read the play, look for reasons why.

CHARACTERS

JODY TIFLIN, a twelve-year-old boy

CARL TIFLIN, Jody's father

MRS. TIFLIN, his mother

LINDA TIFLIN, his sister

BILLY BUCK, a ranch hand

GRANDFATHER, Mrs. Tiflin's father

(*Place: The combined kitchen and dining room of the Tiflin ranch, near Salinas, California.*)

(*Time: Early evening of a windy March day, some years ago.*)

(*Scene: The room is large and rather dull. There is a door in the rear wall, upstage center, leading to the outside. The door itself is open, but there is a screen door, too. Left of the door is a window. A door downstage right leads to the other rooms of the ranch house. Upstage of this door is an old-fashioned kitchen range, with a woodbox on the downstage side of it. Along the wall above the range is a neat array of pots and pans, with a turkey wing for brushing the stove. There is a sideboard for dishes upstage right-center, against the wall. Against the left wall, upstage, is an old-fashioned sink. A towel and a mirror hang above the sink; a wash basin is in the sink. Several dish towels are nearby. Note— if desired, a screen may be placed downstage from the position of the sink and the actual sink eliminated. A small work table is at right center. Left of it is a wooden rocker. Another*) *rocker is at downstage left. At left center, running up-and-downstage, is a long ranch-house table, with benches on both sides and upstage of it. The table is covered with a worn, white oilcloth, and is now set for five for supper. The room is apparently lit by two hanging lamps—one above the long table, the other above the stove.)*

(At the rise of the curtain: The lamps are lit. LINDA *is at the stove, just putting the finishing touches on a large pan of beans for the Tiflin supper.* MOTHER *enters upstage center with a pan of milk. The screen door whips shut behind her.)*

MOTHER *(as she enters).* That wind's getting stronger. Sure no mistake about its being March.

LINDA *(stirring beans).* I thought it might rain. The sun looks leaner every minute.

MOTHER *(as she puts milk on work table, right center, and picks up a broom handle with rope attached).* Who left this old broomstick on my cooking table?

LINDA *(a little disagreeably).* Big Britches! He's making a flail.

MOTHER *(studying broomstick).* A flail?

LINDA. Something to scare mice with. Billy Buck has finished raking the hay—and Big Britches is off on another big plan of chasing the mice out of the remains of the old haystack.

MOTHER *(as she puts flail in woodbox and hands* LINDA *more wood for fire).* Billy Buck shouldn't encourage Jody. Jody should be doing more of the real work on the ranch.

LINDA *(cuttingly).* Well, he's gonna scare mice. . . . When I was twelve I did a full day's work—but Big Britches is gonna scare mice.

MOTHER. You were practical, Linda— *(Pours milk into glasses at work table.)* —but Jody—

LINDA *(breaking in).* Jody is just hungry and impractical. He just ran in—grabbed a big piece of bread, put jelly on it an inch thick—

MOTHER. He'll spoil his supper.

LINDA (*taking napkins from sideboard and placing them around table*). That's all he does—think up ways of wasting his time —spoil his supper—and listen to too many of Grandfather's tales.

MOTHER (*placing glasses of milk on table*). Linda, don't speak of my father in that tone. . . .

LINDA. Oh, I know! Westering was a big thing in Grandfather's life—but— (*Suddenly the door upstage center bursts open and* JODY *dashes in.*)

JODY (*shouting as he bursts in*). Mother! Mother! He's got a letter. (*Crosses to her at table.*)

MOTHER. Jody Tiflin, your hands are all jelly. Wash them this instant; you'll have jelly on everything. (*Pushes him toward sink.*)

JODY (*continuing without interruption*). But he's got—

LINDA (*breaking in*). Quit dragging your feet like that. Shoe leather costs money.

MOTHER. And comb your hair!

JODY (*as he tries to do all these things at once*). He's got a letter!

MOTHER. Who's got a letter?

JODY. Father has! I saw it in his hand when he was riding up. (*Dashes to window.*) Here he is now. (MOTHER *and* LINDA *come to window.* FATHER *is heard outside, as he dismounts from a rather creaky saddle and slaps his horse.*)

FATHER (*offstage*). There you are, Boy! Take her to the barn, Billy.

BILLY (*offstage*). Yes, sir.

JODY (*excitedly*). See the letter! See it! I told you! (FATHER *enters with a letter.*)

MOTHER. (*as* FATHER *enters*). Who's the letter from, Carl?

FATHER (*pausing*). How did you know there was a letter?

MOTHER. Big Britches told us.

FATHER (*a little threateningly, to* JODY, *who tries to make himself as small as possible*). He *is* getting to be a Big Britches—minding everybody's business but his own.

LINDA. Got his big nose into everything.

MOTHER. Well, he hasn't got enough to keep him busy.

FATHER. I'll keep him busy if he don't look out.

MOTHER. Who's the letter from, Carl?

FATHER. I guess it's from your father. Here, read it. (*Hands it to her.* MOTHER *takes a hairpin from her hair, crosses downstage of table, and slits open the flap while others watch intently. Her lips purse judiciously as her eyes snap back and forth over the lines. The others move toward her.*)

LINDA. What does he say, Mother?

JODY (*impatiently*). Yes, what does Grandfather say?

FATHER. Be quiet, Jody! Pile that wood in the woodbox—the pile that's just outside the door. (JODY *gets wood hurriedly from outside door so that he won't miss anything; he takes it to woodbox.*)

MOTHER (*looking up*). He says—he says he's going to drive out Saturday to stay a little while.

JODY (*pausing*). Grandfather—Oh, I hope he hurries!

FATHER (*sternly*). Pile that wood. (JODY *piles wood in woodbox.*)

LINDA. Why, this is Saturday—

FATHER. The letter must have been delayed. (*Crosses to work table and pours glass of water.*)

LINDA (*grabbing envelope to look at postmark*). It should have been here yesterday.

MOTHER (*sternly, to* FATHER). Now, Carl, what have you got that look on you for? He doesn't come often.

FATHER. It's just that he talks—just talks. (*Drinks water impatiently.*)

MOTHER. Well, what of it? You talk yourself.

LINDA (*back at stove, moving hot-water kettle to one side*). But Grandfather only talks about one thing.

JODY (*leaping up from woodbox and barging into* LINDA). Indians! Indians and crossing the plains!

LINDA (*jumping back from stove*). Look here, Big Britches! You almost got me scalded.

FATHER. You get out of here, Big Britches. Go on—get out! (JODY *goes out, taking his flail with him, whipping away at imaginary mice.* FATHER *pours himself another glass of water.*)

LINDA (*dishing beans in bowl on work table*). I've heard that story, about how the horses got driven off, a thousand times —and he never changes a word.

FATHER. *You've* heard it! I heard it ten thousand times before you were born. (*Slams glass on table.*)

MOTHER (*as she rearranges table to make one more place upstage*). That was the big thing in Father's life. He led a wagon train clear across the plains, and when the trip was finished, his life was done. (*Her tone is explanatory.*)

FATHER (*crossing to center*). Well, I can't spend my time listening to it. There are things to be finished on this ranch before *my* life is done. (LINDA *stirs up fire and brushes off stove with turkey wing.* FATHER *washes his hands at sink.* MOTHER *completes setting table through next speeches.*)

MOTHER (*still trying to explain it*). It's a big thing to do, but it didn't last long enough. If there was any farther West to go, he would have gone. (JODY *sticks his head in at the door upstage center and calls excitedly.*)

JODY. He's coming, Mother! He's coming! Can I go meet him?

MOTHER. Yes, go on, Jody. I think he'd like to be met. (JODY *slams door in his excitement.* FATHER *and* LINDA *are annoyed, but* MOTHER *doesn't seem to notice. She continues to explain.*) It's as though he was born to do that, and after it was finished, there was nothing else for him to do but think about it.

LINDA (*maliciously*). And talk about it!

MOTHER. Go meet him, Linda—and be kind. (LINDA *goes out sullenly.*)

GRANDFATHER (*speaking heartily, offstage*). Jody! Come out to meet me, did you?

JODY (*offstage*). Yes, sir. We just got your letter.

MOTHER (*appealingly, to* FATHER). There's nothing for him to do but live by the ocean where he had to stop—and live there with his memories.

GRANDFATHER (*offstage*). Letter should have been here yesterday. Hello, Linda.

LINDA (*offstage*). Hello, Grandfather.

MOTHER (*to* FATHER). Can't you be patient and *pretend* to listen?

FATHER. I'll pretend to listen. Let's go meet him. (MOTHER *and* FATHER *go out.*)

GRANDFATHER (*offstage*). Billy Buck! It's nice to see you, boy. I knew your father.

BILLY (*offstage*). I'll put up your horse, sir.

FATHER (*offstage*). We've been looking for you, sir.

GRANDFATHER (*offstage*). Carl, it's good to see you—and—Daughter—

MOTHER (*offstage*). Do come in, Father. Jody, help with Grandfather's grips.

(JODY *enters with one of* GRANDFATHER'S *grips.* FATHER *comes in, carrying the other grip.* MOTHER *and* GRANDFATHER *come in together, his arm around her shoulder. He is patting her shoulder with his big hand.* JODY *and* FATHER *carry the grips out downstage right.* LINDA *is the last to come in upstage center.*)

LINDA. Let me take your hat, Grandfather— (*Does so.*) --and your walking stick. *(Goes out downstage right with them.)*

MOTHER. Supper's about ready, Father. Would you like to wash up? *(Indicates downstage right.)*

GRANDFATHER. Here at the sink will do. *(Starts to wash hands at sink.)*

MOTHER *(bringing him fresh towel from sideboard)*. How long can you stay, Father? Your letter didn't say.

GRANDFATHER. Well, I don't know. I thought I'd stay about two weeks. *(Shakes water from hands.)* But I never stay as long as I think I'm going to. *(Takes towel.)*

MOTHER *(starting toward door upstage center)*. I must go out and ring the triangle for Billy Buck.

GRANDFATHER *(wiping hands)*. Billy Buck—there's a good boy—

MOTHER *(turning back to door to smile)*. Not much of a boy, Father. Bill's forty-eight. *(Goes out upstage center.)*

GRANDFATHER *(going to door, talking to her as she apparently walks toward triangle)*. I knew the boy's father, Old Mule-Tail. I never knew why they called him Mule-Tail except he packed mules. *(*JODY *hurries in downstage right. Almost without waiting to close the door, he bursts into the adventure which lies nearest to his heart.)*

JODY *(crossing upstage center, practicing with flail)*. Grandfather, would you like to come on a mouse hunt with me tomorrow? Billy Buck's raked the hay and—

GRANDFATHER *(breaking in)*. Mouse hunt, Jody? Have the people of this generation come down to hunting mice?

JODY *(hardly heeding interruption)*. See, I made this flail, and—

GRANDFATHER *(taking flail)*. They aren't very strong—the new people—but I hardly thought mice would be game for them.

JODY *(some of his dream gone)*. No, sir. It's just play. *(Regains a little of the spirit of adventure.)* You see, the mice hide under the soggy hay that's left. And you can watch— *(Makes bribe stronger.)* —or even beat the hay a little.

GRANDFATHER (*a bit teasingly, still occupied with flail*). I see. You don't eat them, then. You haven't come to that yet. (*Outside, the triangle gives the call for supper.*)

JODY (*feeling futility of this empty adventure, taking flail and beginning to wrap rope around handle*). It wouldn't be much like hunting Indians, I guess. (*Crosses to work table right center.*)

GRANDFATHER (*combing his whiskers at mirror above sink*). No, not much. But—later—when the troops were hunting Indians and shooting children, it wasn't much different from your mouse hunt. . . . (*Crosses to him and takes flail.*) After a while, I'll show you the old pistol I used when I led the people across the prairie.

JODY. Oh, Grandfather, I'd love to see it!

GRANDFATHER. Yes, I guess you would. (*Pauses.*) You're really growing up, Jody. You've grown nearly an inch, I should say. (*Measures him with his eye.*)

JODY. More! (*Runs to door downstage right, standing against it.*) See—here, where they mark me on the door. I'm up more than an inch since Thanksgiving.

GRANDFATHER (*studying mark*). Maybe you're getting too much water—and turning to pith and stalk. We'll wait till you head out and see. (*Hands flail back to him.*)

JODY. Grandfather, if I go out right after we eat and make you a flail, will you help hunt the mice tomorrow?

(MOTHER *enters upstage center on* JODY's *speech.*)

MOTHER. Jody, don't bother your grandfather. Call your father and Linda to supper. (JODY *goes out downstage right.*) You sit here, Father. (*Indicates place at upstage end of table.*)

(*As* GRANDFATHER *crosses to the table,* BILLY BUCK *comes in upstage center and goes to the sink to wash his hands.*)

BILLY. I put the horse up, sir.

GRANDFATHER. That's a good boy, Billy. (*Seats himself at upper end of table, facing audience.)* I'm hungry. Driving out here got my appetite up!

BILLY *(wiping hands).* It's the moving around that does it. My father was a government packer. I helped him when I was a kid. We'd get so hungry, we could hardly wait for the meat to get done.

GRANDFATHER. I knew your father, Billy.

BILLY *(going to door upstage center to empty water from basin)* Just the two of us could clean up a deer's ham. *(JODY enters downstage right.)*

JODY *(crossing upstage center).* See my flail, Billy. *(Demonstrates.)* That's to drive the mice out. I'll bet they're fat. I'll bet they don't know what's going to happen to them tomorrow.

BILLY *(philosophically, as he puts basin back into sink).* No, Jody—nor you, either, nor me, nor anyone. *(MOTHER has been bringing food from stove and work table to table left center—the beans, plate of meat, etc. GRANDFATHER is nibbling on a piece of bread.)*

JODY *(crossing to him).* Ought to be plenty mice in that old hay, hadn't there, Billy?

BILLY. Lousy with them. Just crawling with mice—but maybe you better ask your father before you hunt them.

JODY. I don't think he'd care.

BILLY. You'd better ask him. You know how he is. *(He says this a little ominously, as he hangs up towel.)*

JODY *(bravely).* Well, I'll ask him. I'll ask him soon as he comes out.

MOTHER. Be quiet, Jody—and come to the table.

GRANDFATHER *(scarcely realizing that his conversation with BILLY has been interrupted).* Yes, I knew your father, Billy. They used to call him old Mule-Tail. I never knew why, except he packed mules.

(FATHER and LINDA enter downstage right. As they come toward the table, FATHER speaks, a little overzealously.)

FATHER. Well, I hope everyone is hungry. (*They sit down. MOTHER sits at upper right, so that she can be handy to stove. FATHER sits at upper left, opposite MOTHER. LINDA sits next to FATHER. BILLY sits next to LINDA. JODY sits next to MOTHER. FATHER bows his head for a moment, and all follow his example; then, as he looks up, FATHER speaks again.*) Yes, I hope everyone is good and hungry. (*Passes bowl to GRANDFATHER.*) Have some beans, Grandfather.

GRANDFATHER (*as he helps himself and passes bowl on*). I was just telling Billy Boy—driving out here got my appetite up. I like to talk to Billy—Billy hasn't gone soft. (*MOTHER is embarrassed and looks at FATHER menacingly as he fidgets.*)

MOTHER (*to GRANDFATHER, passing bread*). Will you have some bread, Father? (*As the conversation progresses, the clash of generations must be shown in the various attitudes of the people at table.*)

GRANDFATHER (*taking bread without noticing*). I remember the time we ran out of meat. . . . (*Voice drops to a singsong.*) There was no buffalo, no antelope, not even rabbits. . . .

MOTHER. I'll get the tea. (*Rises hurriedly to go to stove; a fork clatters to floor. FATHER bends to pick it up.*)

GRANDFATHER (*continuing*). That was the time for the leader to be on the watch. I was the leader, and I kept my eyes open.

MOTHER (*crossing to GRANDFATHER with teapot*). Will you have some tea, Father?

GRANDFATHER (*holding cup out—never breaking his story*). Know why I had to keep my eyes open? . . . (*Nobody answers; he goes on.*) Well, just the minute the people began to get hungry they'd start slaughtering the team oxen. . . . Do you believe that? (*FATHER looks up toward lamp which overhangs table, rises, and claps his hands together over a moth which is apparently circling it.*)

FATHER. It's a little early for these moths. (*Goes to window, drops moth outside.*)

GRANDFATHER. As I was saying—

FATHER (*as he reseats himself*). You'd better eat your meat. The rest of us will be ready for our pudding and you won't have started. (MOTHER *flashes a warning glance at* FATHER *as she continues around table pouring tea.*)

GRANDFATHER (*without noticing*). I'm pretty hungry, all right. I'll tell you about that later. (*Starts to eat.*)

JODY. Grandfather, will you tell us about the time the Indians— (MOTHER *shushes* JODY. *The others stare him down. Only* BILLY *looks at him with sympathy.*)

MOTHER. Eat your supper, Jody. (*Sits again.*)

GRANDFATHER (*putting down his fork*). I wonder whether I ever told you about those thieving Piutes that drove off thirty-five of our horses?

FATHER (*with deliberate cruelty*). Lots of times! . . . (*Catches* MOTHER's *warning eyes.*) Of course, I'd like to hear it again.

JODY (*braving the displeasure of others, in his eagerness*). Tell us about the Indians, Grandfather.

GRANDFATHER (*his eyes growing stern*). Boys always want to hear about Indians. It was a job for men, but boys want to hear about it.

FATHER (*to* JODY). Didn't your mother tell you to be still? Are you trying to be a Big Britches again?

BILLY (*with understanding, for which* JODY *flashes him a grateful look*). I'd like to hear about the Indians, too, sir.

GRANDFATHER (*turning his attention to* BILLY, *as others eat tensely*). Well, let's see—did I ever tell you how I wanted each wagon to carry a long iron plate?

JODY. No—No, you didn't, Grandfather.

GRANDFATHER. Well, when the Indians attacked, we always put the wagons in a circle and fought from between the wheels. (LINDA *rises to refill water glasses from pitcher on work table. The others give* GRANDFATHER *their attention, though* BILLY *seems more interested in buttering a whole slice of bread.)* I thought that if every wagon carried a long plate with rifle holes, the men could stand the plates on the outside of the wheels—like this— *(Rises and demonstrates with a plate from table.)* —when the wagons were in the circle. and they would be protected. It would save lives and that would make up for the extra weight of the iron. *(Puts plate on table and reseats himself.)* But of course they wouldn't do it. No party had done it before, and they couldn't see why they should go to the expense. *(Takes a bite of meat.)* They lived to regret it, too.

FATHER *(trying to get him off his tangent).* How's the country between here and Monterey?

BILLY *(picking up cue).* I've heard it's pretty dry.

GRANDFATHER. It *is* dry. There's not a drop of water in the Laguna Seca.

FATHER *(continuing his advantage, as he sips his tea).* I hope we get some rain before the crops dry up.

GRANDFATHER *(reminded again).* Well, it's a long pull from '87. The whole country was powder then.

MOTHER *(hastily interposing).* Father, you're scarcely eating a thing.

LINDA *(testily, rattling her fork on plate).* I thought you were hungry.

GRANDFATHER *(not noticing).* And in '61, I believe all the coyotes starved to death. *(Turns to* FATHER.*)* We had fifteen inches of rain already this year.

FATHER. Yes, but it all came too early. We could do with some now. The crops—

GRANDFATHER *(breaking in).* Reminds me of the March in '82. I was leading the people West o—

MOTHER *(as she keeps others in line with her eyes).* Your food is getting cold, Father.

BILLY *(hastily, to keep* GRANDFATHER *from noticing any slights).*

Sir, when you finish your supper, I've got an old powder horn down in the bunkhouse that I'd like to show you . . . or have I shown it to you before?

GRANDFATHER. Yes, you did, Billy. (BILLY *might have saved himself the trouble of protecting* GRANDFATHER'*s feelings; he hasn't noticed anyway.*) Your speaking of that powder horn puts me in mind of a pistol I had when I was leading the people across—

JODY. The one you were telling me about, Grandfather?

GRANDFATHER. Yes, Jody, the very one. *(Starts to rise.)* It's in my grip. I'll get it.

FATHER. Can't it wait until after supper—or tomorrow?

GRANDFATHER. No, I'll get it now. *(Starts toward door downstage right.)*

FATHER. Father, Linda will get it. (LINDA *starts to rise.*)

GRANDFATHER *(motioning* LINDA *to sit down).* No, I know just where to lay my hands on it. I won't be long. *(Goes out downstage right.)*

FATHER *(as door closes behind* GRANDFATHER*).* Billy, I hope you have room in the bunkhouse for me.

MOTHER *(reprovingly).* Carl!

JODY *(staunchly).* I want to hear Grandfather's stories—all of them—after supper.

FATHER. You're going to bed early, Big Britches. You need to be up in the morning.

JODY *(gathering his courage).* Can I hunt the mice in the old haystack, sir?

FATHER. Mice? *(Indulges him.)* Oh, sure! Billy says there isn't any good hay left. You go right after the mice.

JODY *(with a little bravado).* We'll get every one of them tomorrow.

MOTHER *(turning sharply on him).* We! Who are "we"?

JODY. Grandfather and I.

MOTHER. So—you've got him in on it. *(Starts to serve pudding, passing dishes around.)*

LINDA. He always has to have someone in with him to share the blame—if there's blame to share.

FATHER. Well, let Grandfather do it. If he's out hunting mice with Jody, I'll have just that much time off from listening to his stories.

MOTHER *(warningly)*. Don't talk like that, Carl.

LINDA *(to FATHER)*. At least you can stay out in the fields all day.

MOTHER. Linda!

LINDA. Well, it's a fact. I got work to do. I can't spend my time listening to Indian stories. *(Nobody notices that door downstage right has opened slightly.)*

FATHER. He seems a long time coming back. Maybe he can't find the trusty weapon.

BILLY *(anxiously, as he starts to rise)*. He's all right, isn't he? He isn't sick?

MOTHER. I suppose he's taking a minute to spruce up. He likes to comb his whiskers and rub his shoes—and brush his clothes. *(BILLY sits again.)*

FATHER *(cuttingly)*. A man that's led a wagon train across the plains has got to be careful how he dresses.

MOTHER *(with controlled threat)*. Don't talk like that, Carl. Please.

FATHER *(exploding)*. Well, how many times do I have to listen to the story of the iron plate and the thirty-five horses? That time's done.

LINDA. Why can't he forget it—now it's done?

JODY *(in defense of GRANDFATHER)*. I like to hear about it.

FATHER. Be quiet, Big Britches! Why can't he know that that time is over?

LINDA. Why does he have to make us hear it a thousand times?

FATHER. He came across the plains. All right. Now it's finished. (FATHER *and* LINDA *have built on each other's speeches until they seem to be beating down all that* GRANDFATHER *symbolizes. Suddenly, door downstage right closes with a little snap. Everyone at table turns to look at it, horrified. After a moment of terrible silence,* MOTHER *speaks.*)

MOTHER. Carl, he—

BILLY (*almost simultaneously*). Grandfather must have heard.

JODY. Maybe it just shut by itself.

MOTHER. If he heard you, Carl, it will—

(*The door slowly opens,* GRANDFATHER *comes out. He is carrying the pistol.*)

FATHER (*trying to be jovial*). I see you found it.

GRANDFATHER (*dejectedly*). It's just a rusty old piece. Not much good nowadays. (*Puts it on the work table right-center and goes back to table. He sits without speaking further. There is an awkward pause as everyone toys with his food.*)

MOTHER (*after a pause*). Are you ready for your pudding, Father?

GRANDFATHER (*head lowered*). I'm—not—hungry.

FATHER (*blurting it out*). Father—did you hear what I said?

GRANDFATHER (*almost inaudibly*). Yes.

FATHER. I don't know what got into me. I didn't mean it. . . . I was just being funny.

JODY (*astounded to know that* FATHER *could be wrong about anything*). Is Father being ashamed, Mother?

MOTHER. Hush, Jody!

GRANDFATHER (*still looking at his plate*). I'm trying to get right side up. . . . I'm not being mad. (*There is another awkward pause.*)

MOTHER (*breaking pause*). Father, Carl didn't mean to—

GRANDFATHER (*breaking in gently*). I didn't mind what you said, Carl—but it might be true—and I would mind that.

FATHER. It isn't true—I'm not feeling well—I'm sorry I said it.

JODY. Mother, I never knew Father ever did anything to be sorry for.

LINDA. Be quiet, Big Britches.

GRANDFATHER (*not even hearing* JODY's *interruption*). Don't be sorry, Carl. Maybe you're right. The crossing is finished. Maybe it should be forgotten now.

FATHER (*rising quickly*). I've had enough to eat. I have work to do. (*Goes quickly out upstage center.*)

BILLY (*following* FATHER). I'll go with you, sir. (*Goes out upstage center.* MOTHER *and* LINDA *rise and start carrying dishes to work table.* JODY *and* GRANDFATHER *stay at table, motionless, for a time.*)

MOTHER. Linda, we'll pile the dishes in this pan. There aren't many. (*Piles dishes in pan on work table.*)

LINDA. All right. (*She and* MOTHER *continue to stack dishes, quickly and efficiently.*)

JODY (*after a pause*). Won't you tell any more stories, Grandfather?

GRANDFATHER (*trying to be matter-of-fact about it*). Why, sure, I'll tell them—but only when I'm sure people want to hear them.

JODY. I like to hear them, sir.

GRANDFATHER. Of course you do, but you're a little boy. It was a job for men, but only little boys like to hear about it. (*Rises, looking a little tired.*) I think I'll unpack.

MOTHER. Let Linda and me do it for you, Father. It will just take a minute. Come on, Linda. (*She and* LINDA *go out downstage right.*)

JODY (*after a pause*). Father said we could hunt the mice tomorrow.

GRANDFATHER (*absent-mindedly*). That's fine, Jody—real fine. (*Goes to door upstage center and looks into the distance.*)

JODY (*turning around on bench, trying to restore* GRAND-
FATHER'*s old zest*). I'll make a nice flail for you, Grandfather. I'll get up early and make it. You can even use my
stick, if you like.

GRANDFATHER (*hardly knowing* JODY *is in room*). I tell stories
—but they're not what I want to tell.

JODY. I'll paint the stick red for you, Grandfather. Mice really
scamper when they see a red stick. (*Works on his dream.*)

GRANDFATHER. I shouldn't stay, feeling the way I do. I feel as
though the crossing wasn't worth doing.

JODY. You remember Riley—the big boar, sir?

GRANDFATHER (*still not hearing him*). I tell those stories, but
they're not what I want to tell. I only know how I want
people to feel about them. It wasn't Indians that were important.

JODY. I rode Riley sometimes—and he didn't mind.

GRANDFATHER. It wasn't even getting out there that was important. It was the whole bunch of people made into one big,
crawling beast. And I was the head. It was Westering and
Westering.

JODY. Well, Riley ate a hole into that same haystack, and it fell
down on him and smothered him.

GRANDFATHER (*turning to* JODY). Everyone wanted something
for himself, Jody—but the big beast that was all of them
wanted only Westering. I was the leader. (*He says this
proudly; then realization comes.*) But if I hadn't been there,
someone else would have been the head . . . the thing had to
have a head. (JODY *likes to hear about Indians, but this is a
little deep for him; he is as intent on his own dream as*
GRANDFATHER *is on his. Excitement builds for each during
next speeches.*)

JODY. I'll bet you can show me a lot about hunting mice, Grandfather.

GRANDFATHER (*at center stage*). Under the bushes, the shadows were black at white noontide. When we saw the mountains at last—we cried—all of us. It wasn't getting there that mattered. It was movement and Westering.

JODY. Maybe watching them scurry out won't be like chasing Indians—but we can pretend—

GRANDFATHER. We carried life out there—and sat it down—the very way ants carry eggs—and I was the leader.

JODY. —And the mice can be a herd of elephants—and we have invaded the African Jungle.

GRANDFATHER. The Westering was as big as God—and the slow steps that made the movement piled up and up—until the Continent was crossed.

JODY. —And they'll go charging across the plains—

GRANDFATHER.—Then we came down to the sea—and it was done. (*Seats himself in rocker left of work table, his arms hanging.*) That's what I should be telling, instead of stories.

JODY (*whipping his flail for practice, crossing to him*). Grandfather, you will help me hunt the mice, won't you?

GRANDFATHER. No. Jody, I think I'll just stay in bed—but you hunt the mice. It will be a great adventure

JODY. Adventure?

GRANDFATHER. Yes, but keep it to yourself. It's the doing it that counts. When it's done—it's done. (*Picks up old pistol from work table and studies it.*)

JODY (*crossing back to table left center, putting down flail*). Maybe I won't hunt mice tomorrow. Maybe it isn't important. (*Sits on bench right of table.*)

GRANDFATHER. Doing it is, Jody, but after it's done. . . . (*Puts down his pistol. Both sit looking straight ahead for a moment; then* JODY *speaks.*)

JODY. I could lead the people some day. (*Draws aimlessly on table oilcloth with finger.*)

GRANDFATHER. There's no place to go. . . . There's the ocean to stop you. There's a line of old men, hating the ocean because it stopped them. (*Crosses to* JODY *at table.*)

(LINDA *comes in downstage right.*)

LINDA. Your bed is ready, Grandfather—whenever you want to retire.

(*Takes pan of dishes from work table, goes to sink, starts washing dishes.* MOTHER *comes in downstage right.*)

MOTHER. I hope you'll find everything comfortable. (*She goes to help* LINDA. *Through next speeches, they work at sink.*)

JODY. In boats, I might, sir.

MOTHER (*glancing toward him*). In boats you might what, Jody?

JODY. Lead the people.

LINDA (*swishing her dish towel*). Listen, Big Britches, if you lead yourself around to fill that woodbox—and gather the eggs—it'll be about all the leading you'll want to do.

GRANDFATHER (*upstage of* JODY, *outlining circles on table*). There's no place to go, Jody. Every place is taken. But that's not the worst. Westering has died out of the people. Westering isn't a hunger any more. It's all done. Your father is right. It is finished.

JODY (*after a pause*). I guess I won't hunt the mice tomorrow, Grandfather.

MOTHER. Now you're coming to your senses.

JODY (*after a pause*). Grandfather—I guess—I guess if you'd like some lemonade, I could make it for you.

GRANDFATHER (*looking at his strong old hands for a moment*). That would be nice . . . yes, it would be nice to drink lemonade. (*Sits heavily, upstage of table.*)

JODY (*rising, crossing to* MOTHER). Mother, can I have a lemon to make a lemonade for Grandfather?

LINDA (*tauntingly*). And another lemon to make a lemonade for yourself.

JODY. No. I only want one.

LINDA. Well, Big Britches, you must be sick.

MOTHER. Let him alone, Linda. He wants to do something useful at last. (*To* JODY:) You'll find a lemon on the sideboard. (*To* LINDA:) Linda, go out and bring in those clothes before it rains on them. I'll come help you. (JODY *gets a lemon from sideboard.* LINDA *goes out upstage center.* MOTHER *takes a lemon squeezer from top shelf of sideboard.*) Here's the squeezer. (*Hands it to* JODY *and goes out upstage center.* JODY *starts to make lemonade at work table.* GRANDFATHER *goes up to window and looks out, his back to audience. Now, for the first time, we feel that he is really old. His dreams are gone. His shoulders sag. His old hands hang limply. After a pause, he speaks. His words are barely audible. We begin to hear the lonesome patter of rain against window.*)

GRANDFATHER. No place to go, Jody. No place to go. (*But* JODY *isn't listening. He has forgotten about the Indians—and about the mouse hunt. He is engaged in the very practical business of cutting a lemon to make lemonade as curtain closes.*)

(*Curtain.*)

FOR DISCUSSION

1. To Grandfather, "westering" means more than simply traveling westward. What does it mean to him? Is westering over with, as he says it is, or are some activities in present-day society like westering?

2. Before Jody arrives onstage, the audience can answer a number of questions about him. What are the answers to these three:
    a. How old is Jody?
    b. What does Linda usually call him and what does that nickname mean to you?
    c. What is Jody's attitude toward work?

3. Linda is very critical of both Jody and Grandfather. Can you suggest any reasons for her behavior?

4. What is Father's chief objection to Grandfather's coming? What sort of person is Father? Could he be a leader of the people?

5. How do Grandfather's conversations involving Billy Buck show that Grandfather's mind is not as strong as it once was? What is Billy Buck's relationship to the family?

6. In what way are Jody and Grandfather alike? How is Father different from both of them? At the end of the play, both Jody and Grandfather have changed. Discuss the change in each.

7. An important incident in *The Leader of the People* is quite similar to an important incident in *Sorry, Wrong Number*. Both happen accidentally. What are the two incidents?

8. What does Father do that surprises Jody? Does this act seem to change Jody's attitude toward Father? Explain.

9. Do you think that the stories Grandfather told about his experiences were true or not? Why do you think so? How can we recognize truth when we see it or hear it?

FOR COMPOSITION

1. Early in the play Linda says, "The sun looks leaner every minute." This is her way of saying that the sun is fading, that it is no longer bright. Writers often use this kind of expression to compare what they are describing to something else. (For example, cows and horses might look lean.) They might say that before the storm, the clouds looked like giant puffs of soiled cotton blowing across the sky.

   Write a short paper describing what kind of day it is. Tell what the weather looks like and feels like. You might also want to include what it sounds like or what it smells like.

2. What does "west" mean to you? Think about it for a few minutes and then express your ideas and feelings in a brief poem or composition. If you decide on a poem, you may use either a three-line haiku or something longer.

3. Grandfather's recollection of westering is the kind of thing tall tales used to be made from. Tall tales were common when our country was young. What began as a slightly exaggerated account of an incident became wildly exaggerated as it was retold over a period of time. You have probably heard of such heroes of tall tales as Paul Bunyan, John Henry, and Mike Fink. They were "ring-tailed roarers" who claimed to be "half-horse, half-alligator, with a little snapping-turtle thrown in." Write a tall tale in which you make up the name of the hero or heroine. You may use one of the facts from Grandfather's stories or make up a story of your own.

THE
LEADER

EUGENE IONESCO

translated by
DEREK PROUSE

THE LEADER

Did you ever attend a baseball game or a football game and turn on a portable radio to listen to the game? Sometimes the announcer describing the action makes the game seem much more exciting than it really is. By their own excitement and enthusiasm radio and television announcers can cause listeners and viewers to become enthusiastic.

The Announcer in *The Leader* is describing the approach of some famous man. Listen to the Announcer's words and see what effect they have on the people listening to him. Notice, too, the kinds of actions the Announcer describes.

The playwright has put the listeners right on stage with the Announcer so you can see their reactions. Don't be disturbed if some of the other actions in the play don't seem to make sense right away. The playwright has special ways to say special things. Real life has its odd moments, too.

CHARACTERS

THE ANNOUNCER

THE YOUNG LOVER

THE GIRL-FRIEND

THE ADMIRER

THE GIRL ADMIRER

THE LEADER

(Standing with his back to the public, centerstage, and with his eyes fixed on the upstage exit, the ANNOUNCER *waits for the arrival of the* LEADER. *To right and left, riveted to the walls, two of the* LEADER'S ADMIRERS, *a man and a girl, also wait for his arrival.)*

ANNOUNCER *(after a few tense moments in the same position).* There he is! There he is! At the end of the street! *(Shouts of "Hurrah!" etc. are heard.)* There's the leader! He's coming, he's coming nearer! *(Cries of acclaim and applause are heard from the wings.)* It's better if he doesn't see us. . . . *(The* TWO ADMIRERS *hug the wall even closer.)* Watch out! *(The* ANNOUNCER *gives vent to a brief display of enthusiasm.)* Hurrah! Hurrah! The leader! The leader! Long live the leader! *(The* TWO ADMIRERS, *with their bodies rigid and flattened against the wall, thrust their necks and heads as far forward as they can to get a glimpse of the* LEADER.*)* The leader! The leader! *(The* TWO ADMIRERS *in unison:)* Hurrah! Hurrah!

(Other "Hurrahs!" mingled with "Hurrah! Bravo!" come

from the wings and gradually die down.) Hurrah! Bravo! *(The* ANNOUNCER *takes a step upstage, stops, then upstage, followed by the* TWO ADMIRERS, *saying as he goes:)* Ah! Too bad! He's going away! He's going away! Follow me quickly! After him! *(The* ANNOUNCER *and the* TWO ADMIRERS *leave, crying):* "Leader! Leeader! Lee-ee-eader!" *(This last "Lee-ee-eader!" echoes in the wings like a bleating cry.)* *(Silence. The stage is empty for a few brief moments. The* YOUNG LOVER *enters right, and his* GIRL-FRIEND *left; they meet centerstage.)*

YOUNG LOVER. Forgive me, Madame, or should I say Mademoiselle?

GIRL-FRIEND. I beg your pardon, I'm afraid I don't happen to know you!

YOUNG LOVER. And I'm afraid I don't know you either!

GIRL-FRIEND. Then neither of us knows each other.

YOUNG LOVER. Exactly. We have something in common. It means that between us there is a basis of understanding on which we can build the edifice of our future.

GIRL-FRIEND. That leaves me cold, I'm afraid.

(She starts to go.)

YOUNG LOVER. Oh, my darling, I adore you.

GIRL-FRIEND. Darling, so do I!

(They embrace.)

YOUNG LOVER. I'm taking you with me, darling. We'll get married straightaway.

(They leave left. The stage is empty for a brief moment.)

ANNOUNCER *(enters upstage followed by the* TWO ADMIRERS). But the leader swore that he'd be passing here.

ADMIRER. Are you absolutely sure of that?

ANNOUNCER. Yes, yes, of course.

GIRL ADMIRER. Was it really on his way?

ANNOUNCER. Yes, yes. He should have passed by here; it was marked on the Festival program. . . .

ADMIRER. Did you actually see it yourself and hear it with your own eyes and ears?

ANNOUNCER. He told someone. Someone else!

ADMIRER. But who? Who was this someone else?

GIRL ADMIRER. Was it a reliable person? A friend of yours?

ANNOUNCER. A friend of mine whom I know very well. (*Suddenly in the background one hears renewed cries of "Hurrah!" and "Long live the leader!"*) That's him now! There he is! Hip! Hip! Hurrah! There he is! Hide yourselves! Hide yourselves! (*The* TWO ADMIRERS *flatten themselves as before against the wall, stretching their necks out towards the wings from where the shouts of acclamation come; the* ANNOUNCER *watches fixedly upstage, his back to the public.*)

ANNOUNCER. The leader's coming. He approaches. He's bending. He's unbending. (*At each of the* ANNOUNCER's *words, the* ADMIRERS *give a start and stretch their necks even farther; they shudder.*) He's jumping. He's crossed the river. They're shaking his hand. He sticks out his thumb. Can you hear? They're laughing. (*The* ANNOUNCER *and the* TWO ADMIRERS *also laugh.*) Ah . . . ! they're giving him a box of tools. What's he going to do with them? Ah . . . ! he's signing autographs. The leader is stroking a hedgehog, a superb hedgehog! The crowd applauds. He's dancing with the hedgehog in his hand. He's embracing his dancer. Hurrah! Hurrah! (*Cries are heard in the wings.*) He's being photographed, with his dancer on one hand and the hedgehog on the other. . . . He greets the crowd. . . . He spits a tremendous distance.

GIRL ADMIRER. Is he coming past here? Is he coming in our direction?

ADMIRER. Are we really on his route?

ANNOUNCER (*turns his head to the* TWO ADMIRERS). Quite, and don't move, you're spoiling everything. . . .

GIRL ADMIRER. But even so . . .

ANNOUNCER. Keep quiet, I tell you! Didn't I tell you he'd
promised, that he had fixed his itinerary himself. . . . *(He
turns back upstage and cries:)* Hurrah! Hurrah! Long live
the leader! *(Silence.)* Long live, long live the leader! *(Silence.)* Long live, long live, long live the lead-er!

TWO ADMIRERS *(unable to contain themselves, also give a sudden
cry).* Hurrah! Long live the leader!

ANNOUNCER *(to the ADMIRERS).* Quiet, you two! Calm down!
You're spoiling everything! *(Then, once more looking
upstage, with the ADMIRERS silenced.)* Long live the leader!
(Wildly enthusiastic.) Hurrah! Hurrah! He's changing his
shirt. He disappears behind a red screen. He reappears!
(The applause intensifies.) Bravo! Bravo! *(The ADMIRERS
also long to cry "Bravo" and applaud; they put their hands
to their mouths to stop themselves.)* He's putting his tie on!
He's reading his newspaper and drinking his morning
coffee! He's still got his hedgehog. . . . He's leaning on the
edge of the parapet. The parapet breaks. He gets up . . . he
gets up unaided! *(Applause, shouts of "Hurrah!")* Bravo!
Well done! He brushes his soiled clothes.

TWO ADMIRERS *(stamping their feet).* Oh! Ah! Oh! Oh!
Ah! Ah!

ANNOUNCER. He's mounting the stool! He's climbing piggy-
back, they're offering him a thin-ended wedge, he knows
it's meant as a joke, and he doesn't mind, he's laughing.
(Applause and enormous acclaim.)

ADMIRER *(to the GIRL ADMIRER).* You hear that? You hear? Oh!
If I were king . . .

GIRL ADMIRER. Ah . . . ! the leader! *(This is said in an exalted
tone.)*

ANNOUNCER *(still with his back to the public).* He's mounting
the stool. No. He's getting down. A little girl offers him a

bouquet of flowers. . . . What's he going to do? He takes the flowers. . . . He embraces the little girl . . . calls her "my child" . . .

ADMIRER. He embraces the little girl . . . calls her "my child" . . .

GIRL ADMIRER. He embraces the little girl . . . calls her "my child" . . .

ANNOUNCER. He gives her the hedgehog. The little girl's crying. . . . Long live the leader! Long live the leead-er!

ADMIRER. Is he coming past here?

GIRL ADMIRER. Is he coming past here?

ANNOUNCER *(with sudden run, dashes out upstage).* He's going away! Hurry! Come on!

(He disappears, followed by the TWO ADMIRERS, *all crying "Hurrah! Hurrah!")*

(The stage is empty for a few moments. The TWO LOVERS *enter, entwined in an embrace; they halt centerstage and separate; she carries a basket on her arm.)*

GIRL-FRIEND. Let's go to the market and get some eggs!

YOUNG LOVER. Oh! I love them as much as you do!

(She takes his arm. From the right the ANNOUNCER *arrives running, quickly regaining his place, back to the public, followed closely by the* TWO ADMIRERS, *arriving one from the left and the other from the right; the* TWO ADMIRERS *knock into the* TWO LOVERS *who were about to leave right.)*

ADMIRER. Sorry!

YOUNG LOVER. Oh! Sorry!

GIRL ADMIRER. Sorry! Oh! Sorry!

GIRL-FRIEND. Oh! Sorry, sorry, sorry, so sorry!

ADMIRER. Sorry, sorry, sorry, oh! sorry, sorry, so sorry!

YOUNG LOVER. Oh, oh, oh, oh, oh, oh! So sorry, everyone!

GIRL-FRIEND *(to her* LOVER*).* Come along, Adolphe!

(To the TWO ADMIRERS: *)* No harm done!

(She leaves, leading her LOVER *by the hand.)*

ANNOUNCER *(watching upstage)*. The leader is being pressed forward, and pressed back, and now they're pressing his trousers! *(The* TWO ADMIRERS *regain their places.)* The leader is smiling. While they're pressing his trousers, he walks about. He tastes the flowers and the fruits growing in the stream. He's also tasting the roots of the trees. He suffers the little children to come unto him. He has confidence in everybody. He inaugurates the police force. He pays tribute to justice. He salutes the great victors and the great vanquished. Finally he recites a poem. The people are very moved.

TWO ADMIRERS. Bravo! Bravo! *(Then, sobbing:)* Boo! Hoo! Boo!

ANNOUNCER. All the people are weeping. *(Loud cries are heard from the wings; the* ANNOUNCER *and the* ADMIRERS *also start to bellow.)* Silence! *(The* TWO ADMIRERS *fall silent; and there is silence from the wings.)* They've given the leader's trousers back. The leader puts them on. He looks happy! Hurrah! *("Bravos," and acclaim from the wings. The* TWO ADMIRERS *also shout their acclaim, jump about, without being able to see anything of what is presumed to be happening in the wings.)* The leader's sucking his thumb! *(To the* TWO ADMIRERS:*)* Back, back to your places, you two, don't move, behave yourselves and shout: "Long live the leader!"

TWO ADMIRERS *(flattened against the wall, shouting)*. Long live the leader!

ANNOUNCER. Be quiet, I tell you, you'll spoil everything! Look out, the leader's coming!

ADMIRER *(in the same position)*. The leader's coming!

GIRL ADMIRER. The leader's coming!

ANNOUNCER. Watch out! And keep quiet! Oh! The leader's going away! Follow him! Follow him!

(The ANNOUNCER *goes out upstage, running; the* TWO

ADMIRERS *leave right and left, while in the wings the acclaim mounts, then fades. The stage is momentarily empty. The* YOUNG LOVER, *followed by his* GIRL-FRIEND, *appears left running across the stage right.)*

YOUNG LOVER *(running).* You won't catch me! You won't catch me!

(Goes out.)

GIRL-FRIEND *(running).* Wait a moment! Wait a moment!

(She goes out. The stage is empty for a moment; then once more the TWO LOVERS *cross the stage at a run, and leave.)*

YOUNG LOVER. You won't catch me!

GIRL FRIEND. Wait a moment!

(They leave right. The stage is empty. The ANNOUNCER *reappears upstage, the* ADMIRER *from the right, the* GIRL ADMIRER *from the left. They meet center.)*

ADMIRER. We missed him!

GIRL ADMIRER. Rotten luck!

ANNOUNCER. It was your fault!

ADMIRER. That's not true!

GIRL ADMIRER. No, that's not true!

ANNOUNCER. Are you suggesting it was mine?

ADMIRER. No, we didn't mean that!

GIRL ADMIRER No, we didn't mean that!

(Noise of acclaim and "Hurrahs" from the wings.)

ANNOUNCER. Hurrah!

GIRL ADMIRER. It's from over there! *(She points upstage.)*

ADMIRER. Yes, it's from over there! *(He points left.)*

ANNOUNCER. Very well. Follow me! Long live the leader!

(He runs out right, followed by the TWO ADMIRERS, *also shouting.)*

TWO ADMIRERS. Long live the leader!

(They leave. The stage is empty for a moment. The YOUNG LOVER *and his* GIRL-FRIEND *appear left; the* YOUNG LOVER *exits upstage; the* GIRL-FRIEND, *after saying:)* I'll get you!

(runs out right. The ANNOUNCER *and the* TWO ADMIRERS *appear from upstage. The* ANNOUNCER *says to the* ADMIRERS:)* Long live the leader! *(This is repeated by the* ADMIRERS. *Then, still talking to the* ADMIRERS, *he says:)* Follow me! Follow the leader! *(He leaves upstage, still running and shouting:)* Follow him! *(The* ADMIRER *exits right, the* GIRL ADMIRER *left into the wings. During the whole of this, the acclaim is heard louder or fainter according to the rhythm of the stage action; the stage is empty for a moment, then the* LOVERS *appear from right and left, crying:)*

YOUNG LOVER. I'll get you!

GIRL-FRIEND. You won't get me!

(They leave at a run, shouting:) Long live the leader! *(The* ANNOUNCER *and the* TWO ADMIRERS *emerge from upstage, also shouting:)* Long live the leader! *(followed by the* TWO LOVERS. *They all leave right, in single file, crying as they run:)* The leader! Long live the leader! We'll get him! It's from over here! You won't get me!

(They enter and leave, employing all the exits; finally, entering from left, from right, and from upstage they all meet center, while the acclaim and the applause from the wings becomes a fearful din. They embrace each other feverishly, crying at the tops of their voices:) Long live the leader! Long live the leader! Long live the leader!

(Then, abruptly, silence falls.)

ANNOUNCER. The leader is arriving. Here's the leader. To your places! Attention!

(The ADMIRER *and the* GIRL-FRIEND *flatten themselves against the wall right; the* GIRL ADMIRER *and the* YOUNG LOVER *against the wall left; the two couples are in each other's arms, embracing.)*

ADMIRER and
GIRL-FRIEND. My dear, my darling!

GIRL ADMIRER and

YOUNG LOVER. My dear, my darling!

(Meanwhile, the ANNOUNCER *has taken up his place, back to the audience, looking fixedly upstage; a lull in the applause.)*

ANNOUNCER. Silence. The leader has eaten his soup. He is coming. He is nigh.

(The acclaim redoubles its intensity; the TWO ADMIRERS *and the* TWO LOVERS *shout:)*

ALL. Hurrah! Hurrah! Long live the leader!

(They throw confetti before he arrives. Then the ANNOUNCER *hurls himself suddenly to one side to allow the* LEADER *to pass; the other four characters freeze with outstretched arms holding confetti; but still say:)* Hurrah! *(The* LEADER *enters from upstage, advances downstage to center; to the footlights, hesitates, makes a step to left, then makes a decision and leaves with great, energetic strides by right, to the enthusiastic "Hurrahs!" of the* ANNOUNCER *and the feeble, somewhat astonished "Hurrahs!" of the other four; these, in fact, have some reason to be surprised, as the* LEADER *is headless, though wearing a hat. This is simple to effect: the actor playing the* LEADER *needing only to wear an overcoat with the collar turned up round his forehead and topped with a hat. The-man-in-an-overcoat-with-a-hat-without-a-head is a somewhat surprising apparition and will doubtless produce a certain sensation. After the* LEADER'S *disappearance, the* GIRL ADMIRER *says:)*

GIRL ADMIRER. But . . . but . . . the leader hasn't got a head!

ANNOUNCER. What's he need a head for when he's got genius!

YOUNG LOVER. That's true! *(To the* GIRL-FRIEND: *)* What's your name?

(The YOUNG LOVER *to the* GIRL ADMIRER, *the* GIRL ADMIRER *to the* ANNOUNCER, *the* ANNOUNCER *to the* GIRL-FRIEND, *the*

GIRL-FRIEND *to the* YOUNG LOVER:*)* What's yours? What's yours? What's yours?
(*Then, all together, one to the other:*) What's your name?

(*Curtain.*)

FOR DISCUSSION

1. In the Announcer's opening speech, what are the indications that he is excited?
2. Have you ever had the experience of understanding an event better or enjoying it more because you followed it on radio or TV instead of actually going to see it? Do you think the impression that you get from radio or television is as truthful as the one you get when you are there to see for yourself what is happening? Could it sometimes be *more* truthful or *more* complete?
3. By describing different actions of the Leader, the Announcer makes him appeal to different types of people. Name five things the Leader does, and five kinds of people that might think highly of him because he does these things.
4. We hear of singers and entertainers being called "stars," "box-office idols," or even "teen-agers' idols." Are there any ways in which we would consider them leaders?
5. By making the Leader a man without a head, what is the playwright trying to tell us?
6. What happens when somebody discovers that the Leader does not have a head? How does the author show us that the people in the play do not really care about the kind of leader they have?
7. What happens to the two couples during the course of the play? Does their behavior help us understand their attitude

toward the Leader? Do you think that these couples represent just young people or that they stand for young and old?

8. The Leader in this play has some qualities in common with the Emperor in the famous story, "The Emperor's New Clothes." Do you know this story? In what ways are the Leader and the Emperor alike?

9. Sometimes newspapers and magazines give us ridiculous, unnecessary details about the lives of important people. Eugene Ionesco, the author of *The Leader*, pokes fun at this kind of reporting by having the Announcer tell us that the Leader is bending and unbending, that he is sucking his thumb, and so on. Suppose that a famous young television star comes to town and your local newspaper asks you to interview him. The star likes bubble gum and repeatedly pops gum bubbles while you are trying to question him. You become a little irritated with his lack of courtesy. When you have finished talking to him, should you

    a. Write the story without mentioning the bubble gum?

    b. Mention the bubble gum in passing, but not make it seem important?

    c. Show in your story that the gum popping was rude?

    d. Decide that the star was entitled to his enjoyment, and write about the gum cheerfully and humorously?

Decide on one of these four reactions and be prepared to give reasons for your choice.

FOR COMPOSITION

1. Write a paragraph explaining why you think the Announcer describes the Leader so favorably.

2. *The Leader* was originally written for the stage. If you had an opportunity to produce it on either radio or television, which would you choose? Write a brief paper giving your reasons for choosing one or the other. (Do not use production costs as a reason for your choice.)

3. "Should We Play Follow-the-Leader in Real Life?" Write a composition in which you discuss the advantages and disadvantages of doing so. (In this topic, "the leader" would not have to be a single person. The topic includes following the crowd.)

A SPECIAL ACTIVITY

Select a biography of a leader to read. He can be a leader in any field: medicine, sports, government, entertainment, science, military tactics, etc. As you read the book, list two or three qualities that helped make this person a leader. When everyone has reported to the class the qualities he has discovered, make a comparison of them. Does a leader in one field often have the same qualities as a leader in another?

Be sure that the book you choose is about a genuine leader. He should be someone who influences the actions of others. Your teacher or librarian will help you select a book if you have difficulty finding one.

THE
MEADOW

RAY BRADBURY

THE MEADOW

Some of civilization's best friends are dreamers. The men who first dreamed up the wheel and those who envisioned people hurtling through the air faster than the speed of sound have contributed to progress.

Usually dreamers are confronted by practical men who say, "Your idea will never work." Practical men look at dreams in terms of nuts and bolts and dollars and cents.

In *The Meadow*, a dreamer and a practical man face each other on an appropriate battlefield. The setting is Hollywood, where dreams and dollars often clash.

CHARACTERS

VOICE

DOUGLAS

MAN

SECOND MAN

THOMAS M. SMITH

YOUNG

(Music.)
(Sound: A collapsing wall, followed by another and another: the dull thunder of a city falling into rubble.)
(Music: Night theme.)

VOICE. The world lay in partial ruin.

London had been torn down during the day.

Port Said was destroyed.

The nails were being pulled out of San Francisco.

Glasgow was no more.

It was gone, as they say, forever.

(Music: Out.)
(Sound: One last thunder of collapsing walls, a trickling of sand, a faint clatter of boards.)
(Music.)
(Sound: Footsteps. Slow, halting footsteps on gravel.)

VOICE. Here comes the old man.

He walks along the road toward the ruins.

He is the night watchman.

He unlocks the gate in the barbed wire fence and looks in.
(*Music.*)
(*Sound: Rattling of lock, opening of gate, the wind blowing softly.*)

VOICE. There, in the moonlight, lie London and Moscow and New York.

There, in the moonlight, lie Port Said, and Johannesburg and Dublin.

And Stockholm and Provincetown and Clearwater, Kansas.
(*Sound: The wind.*)

VOICE. Just this afternoon it happened. The old man saw it happen.

He was there.
(*Sound: Car drives up. Stops.*)

VOICE. He saw the car drive up outside the barbed wire fence.

And he saw the men in that car.

The fat, bald men with the rich cigars

And the loud sport coats and the new riding breeches

And the riding crops in their hands.
(*Sound: Car doors open and close.*)

DOUGLAS. There it is, gentlemen. Look at it. It's a mess.

MAN. It sure is, Mr. Douglas.

SECOND MAN. Yes, sir.

DOUGLAS. It'll have to go. All of it. It'll have to go.

MAN. You're right, Mr. Douglas. It sure will.

DOUGLAS. What *good* is it? It's no good any more. Look what the weather's done to it.

MAN. It's pretty bad, all right.

DOUGLAS (*thinking*). We—we *might* save Paris. I—don't know.

MAN. Yes. It's not in quite such bad shape, Mr. Douglas.

SECOND MAN. That's right.

DOUGLAS. But—on the other hand—look what the rain's done! That's Hollywood for you. Waste!

MAN. Sure. That's Hollywood for you, Mr. Douglas.

DOUGLAS. Tear it down. Tear it *all* down! Clear it out! We can use that land; it's worth money now. Send a crew of wreckers in this afternoon. Get 'em started.

MAN. Sure thing, Mr. Douglas.

SECOND MAN. Yes, Mr. Douglas.

(*Music: Night theme.*)

VOICE. Now it is night,
The old man stands inside the gate,
It is quiet, except for the wind.
He remembers the car driving off, shining in the sun, this noon.
He remembers what happened this same afternoon
When the wreckers came. . . .

(*Sound: A hammering, ripping, a collapsing of walls.*)

VOICE. When London fell!

(*Sound: Repeat pattern, intensified.*)

VOICE. And New York came down in heaped ruin!

(*Sound: Pattern further intensified.*)

VOICE. And the whole world shook as town after town after town was destroyed!

(*Sound: One last shuddering thunder of falling walls. The wind, in again, sighing.*)

VOICE. The night watchman stands within the barbed wire fence.
He carries a tool chest in one ancient, wrinkled hand.
In his other hand he carries a lunch box.

(*Music.*)

VOICE. Now he walks forward slowly, along the ruined street.
And one moment he is in Baghdad,
And beggars loll in wondrous filth,
And women with sapphire eyes give veiled smiles
From high slim windows.

(*Music.*)

(Sound: The wind.)

VOICE. But it is all strutworks, *papier-mâché*, painted canvas,
Props all lettered with the name of the Studio.
There is nothing behind any of the building fronts,
Nothing at all.
(Sound: Footsteps. A clattering of boards.)

VOICE. The old man now puts down his lunch box and tool chest.
Out of the chest he takes a hammer and some nails.
(Pause.)
(Sound: Boards moving.)

VOICE. He looks about amid the ruin until he finds a few good
strong boards and some canvas.
And he takes the nails in his blunt fingers, and they are
single-headed nails.
And he begins to put London back together again,
Hammering, hammering. Board by board. Wall by wall.
(Sound: A hammering, a slow, patient hammering. A shift-
ing of canvas walls, and an insistent steady slow hammering,
building and building, louder and louder.)
(Music: Picks up effect of sound pattern.)

YOUNG *(in distance, shouts).* Hey, there! Hey, thère, you!

SMITH *(old man).* Uh?
(Sound: After pause, hammering starts again, slowly, cer-
tainly.)

YOUNG. Hey, night watchman. *(Distantly.)* Hey, what's your
name? *(Now coming up.)* Hey, pop, what's your name?

SMITH. Smith. Name's Smith.

YOUNG. Okay, Smith; what's the idea?

SMITH. Who are *you?*

YOUNG. Young. I'm foreman of the wrecking gang.

SMITH. You mean, tearing all this down? I thought you'd done
enough for one day. Why aren't you home, bragging about
it?

YOUNG. There was some machinery over on the Singapore set I had to check. (*Irritated.*) Now, just what do you think you're doing there, Smith?

SMITH. What does it look like I'm doing?

(*Sound: Hammering continues all through above and below.*)

YOUNG. Don't get hot with me, grandpa. I see what you're doing. Put down that hammer. What's the big idea?

SMITH. You just run on, young man, you just run on and let me be. What I do is my business.

YOUNG. You're putting it all up again. We tear it down and you put it up. You crazy?

SMITH. Maybe I am. *Somebody* has to put it up again.

YOUNG. What'd you say your name was?

SMITH. Thomas M. Smith.

YOUNG (*writing*). Smith. Thomas M. Okay. *There.*

SMITH. Writing my name down, are you?

YOUNG. Look, pop, I don't want any trouble. I do my work; you do yours. But I can't have you messing things up, see? I'm turning you in to Mr. Douglas.

SMITH (*hammering steadily*). Send him around. Call him up. I want to talk to him. He's the crazy one. Call him up. Ask him to come see me.

YOUNG. Are you kidding? Douglas don't see *nobody.* (*Laughs.*) I'll call him, sure. Hey . . . (*Suddenly discovers something.*) What *kind of nails* are you using there? (*Angrily.*) *Single* heads! Now, *cut that!* It'll be the very devil tomorrow, trying to pull 'em out.

SMITH. You can't put the world together with double-headed nails. They're too easy to yank out. You got to use single-headed nails and hammer 'em way, way in. Like *this!*

(*Sound: Hammering.*)

YOUNG. I'll give you one more chance. Quit putting things back together and I'll play with you.

SMITH. Young man . . .

(Sound: Hammering in background, as if heard at a distance.)

SMITH. I was here long before you were born. I was here when all *this*—was only a meadow. And there was a wind set the meadow running in waves. For more than twenty years I watched it grow, until it was all of the world, together. I lived here with it. I lived nice. This is the *real* world. That world out there, beyond the fence, is where I spend some time. I got a little room on a little street, and I see headlines and read about wars and strange bad people. But here—here I have the whole world together, and it's peace. I been walking through the cities of *this* world twenty-five years. Any night I feel like it, I have a one o'clock snack at a bar on the Champs Elysées! I can get me some fine Amontillado sherry at a sidewalk cafe in Madrid, if I want. Or else me and the gargoyles, high up there—you see them? On top Notre Dame? We turn over great state matters—and reach big political decisions!

YOUNG. I'm not interested.

SMITH. And now you come and tear it all down and leave only that world out there! That wrong world beyond the fence! You tear all this down and there's no peace any more, anywhere. You and your wreckers, so proud of your wrecking. Pulling down towns and cities and whole lands!

YOUNG. A guy's got to live. I got a wife and kids.

SMITH. That's what they all say. They got wives and kids. And they go on, pulling apart, tearing down, killing. They had orders. Somebody told them. They got to do it.

YOUNG. Shut up, and gimme that hammer.

SMITH. No.

YOUNG. I'm tired of listening to your gaff. *(Deadly.)* Hand it over.

SMITH. Don't come near me.

YOUNG. You think I'm scared of an old fool like you?

SMITH. Don't come any closer!

YOUNG. Why, you poor old crazy coot, I'll . . .

SMITH. I warn you! Stop! This hammer's good for more than nails! I'm warnin' you. Keep your hands off me.

YOUNG. You're insane. (*Pause.*) I'm calling the little white wagon for you, mister. I'm calling the little white wagon. We'll have some of the cops over from the main Studio before the night's over. They'll take you along in a strait jacket. Why—why, you might be a murderer, or—or a fire-bug. Why, you might burn this *whole place up!*

SMITH (*laughs bitterly*). I wouldn't hurt one piece of it!

YOUNG. If you weren't so old . . . (*Backing off.*) Well, you just wait right there, old man, till I get back with the cops.

SMITH. I'm not going anywhere. I'll be right here, building.

YOUNG (*patronizingly*). Yeah. Yeah, *that's* it. Build. Go ahead. Build. Build your darn fool head off. So long, pop!

(*Sound: Running footsteps off, between silent buildings.*)
(*Music: Night theme.*)
(*Sound: Hammering—which then stops abruptly.*)

SMITH. It's no use! (*Exhausted.*) It's no use. I can't put it all back up before they come to take me away. I need help. (*Brokenly, tiredly.*) I need so much help I don't know what to do. There's nothing I can do.
(*Music: Walking theme.*)

SMITH. Make my last rounds. One last good look. Say good-bye to everybody. I'm—crazy. They *say* I'm crazy, anyway. Walk. (*Sound: Footsteps—slow, dragging, tired.*)

SMITH. Shadows all around. All through the world. Shadows of all kinds, sizes. Shadows of buildings. Shadows of people. I don't look right at them. If I look at them—they go away. They disappear. No. I just walk. Down the middle of Piccadilly Circus (*Footsteps.*) . . . or the Rue de la Paix (*Footsteps.*) . . . or Fifth Avenue . . . and I don't look right or left. *(Slow footsteps.)* And all around me, in doorways and in windows, are my friends. *(Footsteps.)* . . . The Russians, singing to the music of their balalaikas. *(Calls.)* Hello-o-o, there! *(Footsteps.)* Spanish gypsies, sitting around a camp-fire. *(Footsteps.)* Shadows. And people. And voices. Just the wind? No, they're *here*. They've been here all these years. And—tomorrow? They—*won't* be here!

(Music: Out.)

(Sound: Horn blowing, far away.)

VOICE. Outside the barbed wire gate stands the Enemy!

Outside the gate is a small black police car

From the Studio itself, three miles away, in town!

(Sound: The horn blaring, off.)

VOICE. The old night watchman stands, transfixed.

He looks to left and right. He does not know which way to run.

There is no place to hide.

None of the buildings is solid.

There is no direction to go except—except UP!

(Sound: The horn again, off.)

VOICE. Up!

(Sound: Horn blares insistently, but still off.)

(Sound: Panting. Footsteps stumbling, climbing ladder.)

VOICE. The old man climbs the ladder. The horn stops blowing.

The gate is being opened! The enemy is in sight.

(Sound: Rattling of chains, off. Bursting open of gate, off.)

MAN *(off, shouts)*. There he goes! There's the night watchman!

SMITH *(panting)*. Won't catch—me. Won't. Won't!

(Sound: Climbing ladder, a rising of wind.)

VOICE. The glaring lights of the police car shine in upon the cities of the meadow, the world.

They reveal the stark canvas set-pieces of Manhattan, Chicago, and Chungking in a bright instant!

The light shines on the imitation stone towers of Notre

Dame Cathedral.

If you look closely, you can see a tiny figure climbing.

Climbing up the ladders and walking along the catwalks of Notre Dame!

Climbing and climbing. Up where the wind is . . .

Up where there is safety, an old man climbs.

SMITH *(panting)*. They—won't— get—me—here.

(Sound: Footsteps below, scuffling, running.)

MAN *(calling up)*. Come down from there, you!

SECOND MAN. Okay, Smith, come on down, come on, now!

SMITH *(panting, climbing)*. No! No, I won't. I won't come down!

MAN *(calling up)*. Save yourself a lot of trouble, Smith! Come on!

(Sound: The wind whining through the strutworks to end of scene.)

SMITH *(calling down, tiredly)*. No. Go get your big producer; see if he can make me come down!

MAN *(calling up)*. All right. If you won't come down, we'll come up after you!

SMITH. Try to come up that ladder and I'll drop one of these gargoyles down on you!

MAN *(calling up)*. We know how you feel, Smith. Hard luck, we know, losing your job, because they're shutting down this place, but. . .

SMITH. You know *nothing!* (Pause.) Listen! *(Gasps.)* You— you want to know how to get me down out of here?

MAN *(pause)*. Sure. How?

SMITH. Get Mr. Douglas over here!

MAN. What?

SMITH. You heard me. Get Mr. Douglas over here and I'll come down.

MAN. We can't do that. Mr. Douglas is a busy man.

SMITH. Get him over here or, before you can stop me, I'll burn this whole place down. I know 'this place better than you; I can get around. Get Mr. Douglas over here!

SECOND MAN *(below)*. Don't argue with him. He's insane. Get Douglas over here pronto. If he wants Douglas, he gets Douglas.

SMITH *(chuckles, speaks to himself)*. I knew that would get them moving. Now—I'll just—take this match and *(Strikes it.)* and—light my—cigar. *(Puffs.)*

(Music: Night theme.)

MAN. There he is, Mr. Douglas; up on top of the Notre Dame set over there.

DOUGLAS. What's he want with me? *(Calls up.)* Hey there, *you!* What do you want with me? Hey, up there!

SMITH *(calling down, from distance)*. Come on up. I want to have a talk with you.

MAN. Don't do it, Mr. Douglas. He's crazy.

SMITH. Bring a gun with you if you want. *(Calling down.)* I just want a little talk with you.

MAN. Don't do it, Mr. Douglas.

DOUGLAS. Don't tell *me* what to do. I'm going up.

MAN. Take my gun then, Mr. Douglas. Do that much, at least.

DOUGLAS. All right, give it to me. Let's get this over with. There's a party I'm supposed to be at in an hour. I'll go part way up and keep under cover. You have your guns ready. I don't want that set burned down or anything. Material's too scarce. We're going to break up that set and use it over at the other lot. It's worth money. O.K., keep me covered. I'm on my way.

(Sound: Footsteps, climbing ladder, hold under.)

DOUGLAS *(panting)*. I'm coming, Smith. But my men have got us both covered. So don't try anything.

SMITH *(calling)*. I won't. Why should I? Just you keep climbing.

(Sound: Climbing ladder again, this time with a little wind

added; then climbing stops. A leg is thrown over the para-pet.)

DOUGLAS *(panting).* All right, Smith. I'm up here. You stay over there where you are. I've got a gun.

SMITH. I'm not afraid of your gun. I won't move. Don't be afraid of me, either. I'm all right.

DOUGLAS. I wouldn't put money on that.

SMITH. Mr. Douglas, did you ever read that story about the man who traveled into the future, two hundred years from now? He found that everybody in that world of the future was insane. Yes, *everybody* was insane. And since everybody was insane, they didn't *know* they were insane. They all acted alike and so they thought themselves normal. And since our hero was the only sane one among them, therefore *he* was abnormal, therefore *he* was insane, to *them* at least. Yes, Mr. Douglas, insanity is relative. It all depends on who has who locked in what cage.

DOUGLAS. I didn't climb up here to talk all night. Get on with it. What do you want?

SMITH. I want a talk with The Creator. That's *you*, Mr. Douglas.

DOUGLAS. Me?

SMITH. Yes, that's you. You're sort of a god. You created all this. You came here one day and struck the earth with a magical checkbook and clapped your hands and said, "Let there be Paris!" And there was Paris: streets, bistros, flowers, and all! You were a god, creating. And you clapped your hands again. You cried, "Let there be Constantinople!" And there *it* was! You clapped your hands a thousand times. Each time you created something new. Now you think you can just clap your hands once more, and it'll all fall down into ruins. But, Mr. Douglas—it's not as easy as that.

DOUGLAS. I own fifty-eight per cent of the stock in this Studio.

SMITH. Did you ever think to come here late some night and climb up here and look and see what a wonderful world you created? Did you ever wonder if it might not be a good idea for you to sit up here with me and my friends, and have a cup of Amontillado sherry with me? All right—so the Amontillado smells and looks and tastes like coffee. Imagination, Mr. Creator, imagination. But no, you never came around; you never climbed up. There was always a party somewhere else. And now, very late, without asking us, you want to destroy it all. You may own fifty-eight per cent of the Studio stock, but you don't own *them!*

DOUGLAS. "Them"? Who in thunder is "them"?

SMITH. Them? It's hard to put in words. People who live here.

DOUGLAS. There are no people here.

(Music: Night theme.)

SMITH. Yes, there are. There were so many pictures made here, in all the years. Extras moved in the streets. In costumes. They talked a lot of languages. They smoked cigarettes and meerschaums and Persian hookahs, even. Dancing girls danced. They glittered. Women with veils smiled from high windows. Soldiers marched. Children played. Knights in armor fought. There were tea shops. People sipped tea in them and dropped their h's. Gongs were beaten. Viking ships sailed the seas.

DOUGLAS. It's cold up here.

SMITH *(going right on).* And, somehow, after the extras went, and the men with the cameras and equipment and microphones—after they all walked away and the gates were closed and they drove off in big limousines, somehow something of all those thousands of people remained. The things they *had been,* or pretended to be, stayed on. The foreign languages, the costumes, the things they did, things they *thought,* their manners and their religions. All those little things stayed on. The sights of far places. The smells. The salt wind. The sea. It's all here, tonight—if you listen.

(Sound: The wind.)

DOUGLAS. Ummm. The wind.

SMITH. You heard! You *did* hear, didn't you? By golly, you did! I see it in your face!

DOUGLAS. Well, if I say so myself, I've got a pretty good imagination! But you should have been a writer. Well, are you ready to come down now?

SMITH. You sound a little more polite.

DOUGLAS. Do I? I don't know why I should. You've ruined a good evening for me.

SMITH. Did I? It hasn't been bad, has it? A bit different, I should say. Stimulating perhaps.

DOUGLAS (*pause*). You're a funny old man. I can't figure you. And I wish I could, somehow.

SMITH. Don't tell me I've got you thinking? You're not as excited as you were.

DOUGLAS. After you've lived in Hollywood long enough, you meet all kinds. Besides, I've never been up here before. But what I'd really like to know is, why you should worry about all this junk. What's it to *you?*

SMITH. I'll show you what it is to me. As I said before, you came here, years ago, clapped your hands and twenty, fifty, one hundred cities appeared. Then you added eighty different nations and a half thousand other people and religions and political setups, inside the barbed wire fence.

DOUGLAS (*mechanically*). And there was trouble.

SMITH. Right. You can't have that many people, crowded so close, and not have trouble. But the trouble died out. You know why?

DOUGLAS. If I did, I wouldn't be standing up here, freezing. (*Music: Night theme again.*)

SMITH. Because you got Boston joined to Trinidad, part of Trinidad poking out of Lisbon, part of Lisbon leaning on Alexandria, Alexandria tacked onto Shanghai, and a lot of little pegs and nails between, like Chattanooga, Oshkosh,

Oslo, Sweet Water, Soissons, Beirut, Bombay, and Port Arthur. You shoot a man in New York and he stumbles forward and drops dead in Athens. You take a political bribe in Chicago and somebody in London goes to jail. You push a knife into a man in Berlin and it comes out the back of a man in Memphis. It's all so close, so very close. That's why we have peace here. We're all so crowded there *has got to be peace*, or nothing would be left. One fire would destroy all of us, no matter who started it, for what reason. So all of the people, the memories, whatever you want to call them, that are here, have settled down, and this is their world, a good world; and tomorrow—you're destroying it. *(Music: Out.)*

(Sound: The wind blows quietly through the struts.)

DOUGLAS *(clears throat)*. Uh. Yes. I see. *(Self-consciously.)* Well. Shall—shall we go down now?

SMITH. Yes, I'm ready to go if you are. You go down first, Mr. Douglas. I know you don't trust me. I don't blame you. You go on down. I'll follow you.

(Sound: Steps going down.)

SMITH *(panting)*. Here we are. *(Pause.)* What—what are you going to do now?

DOUGLAS. Why, I hadn't thought. Go to that party, I suppose.

SMITH. Will it be fun?

DOUGLAS *(not certain)*. Yes. *(Now somewhat irritated.)* Yes! Sure, it'll be fun. *(Pause.)* Don't tell me you've still got that hammer?

SMITH. Yes.

DOUGLAS. You going to start building again?

SMITH. Yes. It won't hurt anything; it's not destructive, is it?

DOUGLAS. I guess I can't object to that. You don't give up, do you?

SMITH. Would you, if you were the last builder and everybody else was a wrecker?

DOUGLAS. I think I know how you feel. Well, maybe I'll see you again, Smith.

SMITH. You won't. I won't be here. This all won't be here. If you come back again, it'll be too late.

DOUGLAS (*uncomfortably*). Oh yes, I forgot. Well. It's nine-thirty. I can't stand here jabbering all night.

SMITH. No, you can't, can you?

DOUGLAS. Don't look at me that way. What do you want me to do?

SMITH. A simple thing.

DOUGLAS. What?

SMITH. Leave all this standing. Leave these cities up.

DOUGLAS. I can't do that.

SMITH. Why not?

DOUGLAS. Blast it, I just can't. Business reasons. It has to go.

SMITH. A man with a really good mind for business could think up a profitable reason for it to stay.

DOUGLAS. You make me sound like a heel.

SMITH. That's for you to decide.

DOUGLAS. Well, my car's waiting. Now how do I get out of here?

(*Sound: A clattering of boards.*)

SMITH. Watch it! That building's falling!

DOUGLAS. (*Cries out.*)

(*Sound: Terrific thunder as building falls.*)

SMITH. Here! This way! Jump!

(*Sound: Building rumbles and falls into silence.*)

SMITH (*gasping*). Are you all right?

DOUGLAS. Yes. (*Breathing hard.*) Thanks. Thanks. You probably saved my life.

SMITH. Hardly that. Those were only *papier-mâché* bricks. You might have been cut a little.

DOUGLAS. Nevertheless, thanks. What building was that that fell?

SMITH. It was a Norman village tower, built in 1925. Don't go near the rest of it; it might collapse.

DOUGLAS. I'll be careful. Why, *(Testing set.)* I could push this—whole *(Grunting.)* thing, this whole building over with one hand.

SMITH. But you wouldn't want to do that.

DOUGLAS. Oh, wouldn't I? And why not? Why should I care? What's one more French house more or less?

SMITH. Here. I'll show you. Walk around to the other side of the house.

DOUGLAS. *(Grunting, walking.)*

(Sound: Their footsteps in rubble.)

SMITH. There. Read the sign on the other side.

DOUGLAS. *(reads).* First National Bank. Mellin Town, *(Pause.)* Illinois.

(A silence.)

(Sound: The wind blows.)

DOUGLAS. On one side—a French tower. On the other, *(Walking in ruin.)* First National Bank. Bank. Tower. Bank. Tower. Hmmm.

SMITH. Still want to push the French tower down, Mr. Douglas?

DOUGLAS. Eh?

SMITH. I said, you still want to. . .

DOUGLAS. Don't bother me. I'm thinking.

(Music: Walking theme.)

DOUGLAS. Eh . . . what . . . what's this, over here?

SMITH. A Chinese pagoda.

DOUGLAS. And inside it?

SMITH. The log cabin where Lincoln was born.

(Sound: The wind. And their footsteps, walking faster and faster.)

DOUGLAS. And *here?*

SMITH. St. Patrick's Cathedral, New York.

DOUGLAS. And inside it?

SMITH. A Russian Orthodox cathedral in Rostov.

DOUGLAS. What's this?

SMITH. That? Don't walk so fast, Mr. Douglas. That? That's a door of a castle on the Rhine!

DOUGLAS. And inside?

SMITH. A Kansas City soda fountain!

DOUGLAS (*with music rising in a tide and drowning and covering his words*). And here? And here? And over here? And here? What's this? What's that? And over there—this and that and this and that. . . .

(*Music: Out.*)

DOUGLAS (*puffs cigarette five seconds*). Here. (*Pause.*) Have a cigarette.

SMITH. Thanks.

(*Sound: Lighting up. Slow puffing.*)

DOUGLAS. You got your hammer?

SMITH (*pause*). Yes, sir.

DOUGLAS. And nails?

SMITH. Yes, sir.

DOUGLAS (*puffs cigarette . . . then speaks quietly*). Put all this together again.

SMITH. What did you say?

DOUGLAS. You heard me. (*Louder.*) Nail it all back up. Give it a coat of paint, if you need to. But nail it all back up. (*Puffing cigarette.*) I think I understand what you meant when you said a man with a really good imagination could think up a way to leave all this up and still make a profit. I know a darned good way.

SMITH (*amazed silence, then incredulous*). You're not—just fooling an old man, are you?

DOUGLAS. With a three-million-dollar investment, I'm not fooling! (*Silence. Cigarette again.*) It'll make a beautiful film, Smith. A beautiful film. We'll make it all here, inside the fence. We'll show it all. We'll photograph all this ten different ways. We've got a story. You gave it to me. It's your idea. We'll put some writers to work on it, good writers. And we gotta get a title for it. Something like *One World*. And when we finish the picture we'll take it out and show it to people everywhere in the world, and they'll like it. They've *got* to like it. They can't pass it up; it's too important. *(Pause.)* Yes, Smith, you've got yourself a new job . . . and so have I. You'll be—technical director on the film. In the meantime, use your hammer. *(Crisply.)* Well, see you tomorrow, Smith. We'll talk some more. And—uh, say, it's cold.

SMITH. Like a drink, Mr. Douglas?

DOUGLAS. Don't mind if I do. Some of that—what did you call it?

SMITH. Amontillado. 1876.

DOUGLAS. Amontillado. That's it. Let's have some of that.

(Sound: Opening of thermos and pouring of liquid.)

DOUGLAS. Thanks. Here's to you. *(Drinks.)* Ah! Good.

SMITH. It might taste like coffee, but I tell you it's the finest Amontillado sherry ever bottled.

DOUGLAS. You can say that again! Well, got to be going. Shake, pop. And—hey! Be careful with that cigarette.

SMITH. Uh?

DOUGLAS. You want to burn down the whole darn world?

SMITH. Eh? *(They laugh together.)* Sure. Sure. I'll be careful!

DOUGLAS. So long, Smith. *(Fading.)* I'm late for that party.

SMITH. So long, Mr. Douglas. So long.

(Sound: Footsteps walk off briskly, stop. Gate hasp clicks. Gate opens, closes sharply. Footsteps again. The wind comes up once more.)

FOR DISCUSSION

1. The practical man and the dreamer are often in conflict with each other. In *The Meadow*, who is the practical man? Who is the dreamer? Which one wins the struggle? Is the solution that is agreed on a practical one or a dream? Would you rather be a practical person or a dreamer? Compare the ending of this play with that of *The Leader of the People*.

2. The narrator's voice is heard frequently at the beginning of *The Meadow*, but is dropped before the play is half over. In his descriptions and comments, does the Voice support one side in this conflict, or does he remain uninvolved? What is the narrator's main function? Why do you think the narration was discontinued so soon in the play?

3. As in *Sorry, Wrong Number*, the sounds in *The Meadow* help the listener to picture the setting and to follow the plot. They also help describe the two main characters, Thomas Smith and Mr. Douglas. Which sound effects indicate the kinds of personalities these two men have? What kinds of personalities do they have?

4. Young's reason for tearing the set down is "A guy's got to live. I got a wife and kids." Exactly what does he mean by this statement? What does it tell us about Young? Read all of Young's lines; then decide what attitude Ray Bradbury wants us to have toward Young. Why does the author want us to feel this way?

5. The two men from the studio say virtually the same thing. Why do you suppose the playwright included two of them instead of just one? How would you describe them? What seems to be Mr. Douglas's attitude toward them?

6. During the course of the play, the outlook of one character changes in some respects while the outlooks of the others remain about the same. Which character's outlook changes? In what ways? Which of his old traits does he retain?

7. An important element in *The Meadow* is the theme or idea it presents. What is the theme of the play? How does the title tie in with this theme?

FOR COMPOSITION

1. Mr. Douglas decides to write an inter-office memo to his staff, telling of changes in plans for the sets in the meadow. The teacher will divide your class into two groups. Group 1 will write the memo the way Mr. Douglas probably wrote it. Some ideas may not be in complete sentences. There may even be a word or two misspelled. Group 2 will write it the way Mr. Douglas's secretary would type it. Everything should be letter perfect in Group 2's work. Don't make the memo longer than 20 lines.

2. Should the publicity for the movie "One World" emphasize dignity or showmanship? Can the two elements be combined successfully? Decide what the tone should be; then make up a one-paragraph publicity release for the film. You may use the names of movie stars if you like.

3. If Thomas Smith were married, he would probably go home the next morning and talk over the night's events with his wife. Suppose that he is sitting at the table describing what happened while she is preparing breakfast. Suppose, too, that Mrs. Smith is a practical, businesslike woman. Write a page or two giving their conversation. Be sure to indicate sound effects, especially to show Mrs. Smith's activities.

4. Write a short composition on one of these topics:
   a. How Small Is My World?
   b. Three Reasons Why Radio Drama Died
   c. Everyone Was Wrong Except Me

ABOUT THE PLAYWRIGHTS

RAY BRADBURY (1920-   ) is one of America's most respected writers of science-fiction stories. Although his stories are mainly concerned with human beings, they also deal with robots, fantasies, and mental telepathy. Bradbury's message is that mankind will be in trouble if men do not maintain better control of their technological inventions. The most famous collections of such stories are *The Illustrated Man, The Martian Chronicles,* and *The October Country.* He has also written novels, including *Fahrenheit 451* and *Dandelion Wine.* But Ray Bradbury, who has mastered the complicated world of tomorrow in his writings, has never learned to drive a car.

LORD DUNSANY, Edward John Moreton Drax Plunkett (1878-1957), was born in England of Irish parents. Although he was more interested in hunting and soldiering than in writing, he produced novels, poems, and dramas. Lord Dunsany's plays, which have been produced in many countries, deal almost exclusively with "the mysterious kingdom where geography ends and fairyland begins." *The Jest of Hahalaba* is typical of his plays in that it centers around a supernatural event. Others of his famous plays are *A Night at the Inn* and *The Lost Silk Hat.*

LUCILLE FLETCHER (1913-   ) is a native of Brooklyn, a graduate of Vassar, and a member of Phi Beta Kappa, the national honorary society for people who compile outstanding scholastic records in college. She has had the happy experience of seeing her radio play *Sorry, Wrong Number* become a stage play, a novel, a television play, and a motion picture. In addition to writing dramas of suspense, she has written a mystery novel and made contributions to many magazines.

ALICE CHILDRESS was born in Charleston, South Carolina, and was raised in Harlem in New York City. During the twelve years she spent with the American Negro Theater, she was a drama coach, director, writer, and actress. Her play, *Wedding Band,* was selected by the University of Michigan for presentation at their Professional Theater Program New Play Project in 1966. It starred Ruby Dee and Abby Lincoln. This play was also produced in February, 1969, at the new municipal theater in Atlanta, Georgia. Recently, she finished her second and final year of a Harvard appointment at the Radcliff Institute for Independent Study where she completed the book for a new musical play, *The African Garden.* Her husband Nathan Woodard wrote the music. Miss Childress is now working on a compilation of plays by black playwrights for junior high school students and is writing *Young Martin Luther*

King, a play scheduled to tour high schools. Miss Childress is a member of The New Dramatists Committee.

JAMES ENE HENSHAW (1924–   ) was born in Eastern Nigeria. After attending college in Africa, Henshaw went to Dublin, where he earned a degree in medicine. *The Jewels of the Shrine* was awarded a first prize in a Nigerian festival in 1952 and has been extremely popular with African drama students ever since. Although Dr. Henshaw spends most of his time on his medical activities, he continues to write plays.

HOLWORTHY HALL (1887-1936; the pen name for Harold Everett Porter) and ROBERT MIDDLEMASS (1884-1949) were friends who collaborated on *The Valiant* shortly after the end of the first World War. According to one account, Middlemass actually wrote the play himself, and gave it to his friend because Porter needed some material to meet a publisher's deadline. The pseudonym *Holworthy Hall* was taken from the name of a Harvard dormitory. *The Valiant* was first published in 1921, and over the years has become one of the most popular one-act plays in the history of the American theater.

EUGENE IONESCO (1912–   ) was born in Roumania. From 1913 to 1925 he lived in Paris and in 1938 he became a French citizen. Ionesco taught French and served as a literary critic before his first play was published in 1950. Most of his plays are very unconventional, as one might guess from titles such as *The Bald Soprano* and *Rhinoceros.* He is one of the foremost writers in the modern theater movement called the "theater of the absurd."

ROBERT EMMET SHERWOOD (1896-1955) was awarded three Pulitzer Prizes for drama within a five-year period. The prizes were given to him in 1936, for *Idiot's Delight;* in 1939, for *Abe Lincoln in Illinois;* and in 1941, for *There Shall Be No Night.* Although Sherwood also wrote plays for television and motion pictures, his greatest dramatic triumphs were in the theater. *Abe Lincoln in Illinois* is usually considered his most successful play. He won a fourth Pulitzer Prize in 1949 for his biography, *Roosevelt and Hopkins.*

JOHN STEINBECK (1902–1968) worked in California as a hod carrier, painter, laboratory assistant, ranch hand, and fruit picker, and drew upon many of his experiences when writing his widely-acclaimed novels and short stories. His work has been translated into more than thirty languages. Among his most successful books are *Of Mice and Men* (1937), *The Grapes of Wrath* (1939), and *The Pearl* (1948). *The Grapes of Wrath* was awarded a Pulitzer Prize in 1940. Steinbeck received the Nobel Prize for literature in 1962.

GLOSSARY OF TERMS USED IN PLAY PRODUCTION

THE STAGE

UPSTAGE RIGHT	UPSTAGE CENTER	UPSTAGE LEFT
RIGHT	CENTER	LEFT
DOWNSTAGE RIGHT	DOWNSTAGE CENTER	DOWNSTAGE LEFT

WINGS *(offstage)* — left side

WINGS *(offstage)* — right side

CURTAIN

AUDIENCE

close-up: A camera shot made with the camera close to an object or person. The shot reveals little or no background.

dolly after: To move the television or motion picture camera toward an object.

dolly back: To move the camera away from an object, by rolling back the small, wheeled cart the camera rests on. The term *dolly* refers to the cart.

dissolve to: To change one scene into another by gradually blurring the image of the first scene and clarifying the image of the second. Dissolves are used to create a slow change of mood in both movies and television.

hold under, as in *(Sound: Footsteps, climbing ladder, hold under):* To continue the sound effect, with less volume, while the dialogue proceeds.

off, as in *(Sound: The horn again, off):* Offstage. The sound comes from a place where the characters are not performing.

GLOSSARY OF THEATER TERMS

action: the happenings—psychological, emotional, and physical—that convey the meaning and story of the play.

antagonist: the force (usually a person) that opposes the main character (the protagonist) in his attempt to solve a problem and thus resolve the conflict in which he is involved.

anticlimax: an outcome of a situation or series of events that, by contrast with what was anticipated, is ludicrous or disappointing. The anticlimax can often create a humorous effect.

atmosphere: the general, over-all feeling of a literary work conveyed in large part by the setting and the mood.

characterization: the development of a character through what he says and does and through what other characters say about him.

climax: the moment of greatest dramatic intensity; the turning point in the action, usually followed by a decrease in suspense.

comedy: a form of drama that is light and amusing and typically has a happy ending. Many comedies poke fun at—satirize—manners, customs, social or political institutions or types of people.

conflict: the struggle between two opposing forces, ideas, or beliefs, which is the basis of the plot. In most plays the conflict is resolved when one force—usually the protagonist—succeeds or fails in overcoming the opposing force. Sometimes, the protagonist gives up the struggle as too difficult or not worthwhile. The term *inner conflict* refers to a struggle within the heart and mind of the protagonist. The term *external conflict* refers to a struggle between the protagonist and an outside force.

denouement: the unraveling of the plot, following the climax, in which the writer explains how and why everything turned out as it did.

dialect: the speech that is characteristic of a particular region or of a class or group of people.

dialogue: the conversation between two or more characters in a play.

dynamic character: one who undergoes some change during the course of the play.

episode: an event, or set of events, that helps to make up the main plot or, at times, is incidental to it.

exposition: the background information that reveals "how it all began"; namely, what happened prior to the time covered in the play, what the main characters are like (sometimes before they appear), and what situation has arisen that will lead to a problem that must be solved.

falling action: the action following the climax; also referred to as *resolution* or *denouement*.

fantasy: a play involving such unreal characters and improbable events that the reader is not expected to believe it. Some fantasies are intended merely to entertain; others have a serious purpose as well; namely, to poke fun at outmoded customs or at the stupidity of certain people or groups of people.

flashback: a dramatic device by which the playwright interrupts the main action of the play to present a situation or incident which occurred at an earlier time.

foreshadowing: the dropping of important hints by the author to prepare the reader for what is to come and to help him to anticipate the outcome.

incident: one of the events (usually minor) that make up the total action or plot of a drama.

irony: a mode of expression in which the author says one thing and means the opposite. The term also applies to a situation, or the outcome of an event (or series of events), that is contrary to what is naturally hoped for or expected.

locale: the particular place in which the action in a play occurs.

mood: the frame of mind or state of feeling created by a play; for example, a *skeptical* mood or a *sentimental* mood.

motivation: the cause or reason that compels a character to act as he does.

plot: the series of events or episodes that make up the action of a play.

protagonist: usually the main character, who faces a problem and, in his attempt to solve it, becomes involved in a conflict with an opposing force.

resolution: the events following the climax of a play; it is sometimes called *falling action.*

rising action: the series of events, preceding the climax, which intensify the conflict and, thereby, create a feeling of suspense about the outcome.

scene: a short episode in which the time, and possibly the place, are different from that of a previous episode; also, an incident or happening in the play that develops naturally out of the preceding action and flows into the action that follows.

setting: the time and place in which the events in a play take place.

stage directions: the words, phrases, sentences, and even paragraphs, printed in italics and enclosed in parentheses, through which the playwright indicates what is taking place on the stage and how he wants the characters to speak, feel, or act. Occasionally, he uses the stage directions to comment on a character or situation or to suggest the particular mood to be created at that point in the play.

static character: one who undergoes little if any change during the course of the play.

theme: the idea, general truth, or commentary on life or people brought out through the play.

tone: the feeling conveyed by the author's attitude toward his subject and the particular way in which he writes about it.

tragedy: a form of drama in which the protagonist undergoes a morally significant struggle and is defeated, sometimes because of a flaw in his own character, more often because he is unable to overcome the force, or forces, that oppose him.

unity: the quality in a play that gives it the effect of being a harmonious whole.